'In April' Geoffrey Chaucer tells us, 'folk long to go on pilgrimages'.

I've never met ANYBODY who longed to go on a pilgrimage. For years baffled by this outrageous calumny, I finally realised, one intoxicating April day, what he meant. For pilgrimages, read explorations. Folk – lots of folk – long to go on explorations. A sentiment echoed centuries later by a famous bear who loved his 'expotitions', and expressed to perfection by an equally famous toad:

"The open road, the dusty highway, the heath the common, the hedgerows, the rolling downs! Camps, villages, towns, cities! Here today, up and off to somewhere else tomorrow! Travel, change, interest, excitement! The whole world before you, and a horizon that's always changing!"

Exploring holidays can last a weekend or a lifetime, encompassing a satisfying clutch of cliches.

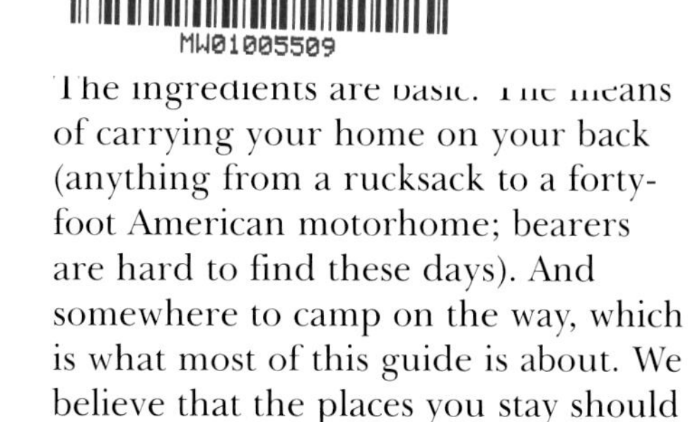

you

The ingredients are basic. The means of carrying your home on your back (anything from a rucksack to a forty-foot American motorhome; bearers are hard to find these days). And somewhere to camp on the way, which is what most of this guide is about. We believe that the places you stay should crown the experience of exploring, not compromise it. And that each one should be a discovery in its own right.

There is no finer feeling, come April or any other time, than to set off to see where your journey takes you. For the pilgrims, the Poohs, the Toads and all the other wanderers and wonderers of this world, this book is written.

Make sure you know the rules of the road in the country you're exploring.

Non-native motorists may regard driving on the left as typically British bloody-mindedness, probably correctly. This perversion apart, though, complications are few. These islands are blessed with reasonable – though heavily-used – roads, free motorways and (mostly) careful, considerate drivers. All the rules, speed limits, road signs and regulations can be found in 'The Highway Code'; this little booklet is easily found in newsagents and bookshops and is indispensible. A few special reminders, though, for towers and tourers:

- ***Keep left – and go clockwise on roundabouts***
- ***Beware congested town centres***

- ***Height restricting car park barriers are common***
- ***On motorways, towed units must not exceed 60 m.p.h. and, where there are three lanes, must not use the outside one***

- ***Do not tow more than the appropriate weight for your car***
- ***Travelling in the back of a motor caravan? Wear seatbelts***

- ***Turn off gas in tunnels and on ferries***
- ***Tolls are payable for some bridges and road tunnels***

- ***Don't park dangerously or without lights at night***

- ***Carry proof of insurance***

IN EMERGENCY – use roadside phones on motorways, or phone 999 (free call) for police, fire service or ambulance.

Get Organised - Get Equipped

Preparing for trips is very much part of the fun. A well-mounted expedition creates comfort, minimises time-wasting and makes for voluptuous smugness.

Truly macho real explorers will of course protest here and mutter on about building a shelter for ten with two oak leaves and a sheepshank in the Boy Scouts. They have a point; travelling light can be intoxicating in the sense of freedom it brings. Witness though the other approach, the Doctor Livingstones and Hannibals, mounting their expeditions with enormous entourages, big budgets and odd definitions of essential. Happiness, surely, lies somewhere between the two.

A useful equipment checklist, for you to scorn or augment according to your style, follows shortly. First, though, you will need a tent, a caravan or a motor caravan, your own or hired, in order to carry your home on your back. (Usually at this point in these things snails get a mention, rather irrationally. You do NOT need something slow, aerodynamically disastrous and with – presumably – little storage space).

If you don't already own your equipment, you must decide which of these three options best suits you, your circumstances and your bank manager. This is a realm of irreconcilable camps and strong passions. Real explorers do it in tents, says one faction (prize, by the way, for the best printable suggestion for what follows 'Real Explorers do it .....' on the inevitable car sticker). Owners of towed caravans, and those of the self-propelled alternatives, smile gently at each other with an air of trying to humour the sadly misguided.

Not for us, but for the experts, to present the rival contestants!

Checklist

- Bedding, linen, towels, tea towels, cloths
- Crockery, cutlery, kitchen utensils, pots and pans
- Food, cleaning materials, washing-up liquid, loo rolls
- Rubbish bags, hose, garden furniture
- Clothes, shoes, boots, waterproofs, toiletries
- Prescriptions, drugs, medications, first aid supplies
- Torch, penknife, string, matches, safety pins, superglue
- Stationery, stamps
- Books, magazines, music, games, toys, quizzes
- Barbecue and equipment
- Bikes, puncture repair outfit, tools
- Maps, compass
- Phonecard, small change or mobile phone
- Vehicle documents, insurance details

MARQUIS MOTORHOMES
Winchester Road
Lower Upham, nr
Southampton
Hampshire SO32 1HA
Tel: 01489 860 666
Fax: 01489 860 752

"Surely there is no better way for the intrepid traveller to explore Britain and beyond than from behind the wheel of a motorhome! Go where you want, when you want – all in 5-star luxury!

Even if you've never been in a motor caravan before, life behind the wheel of your mobile 'holiday home' couldn't be simpler. Power steering makes them easy to drive, and diesel engines make them economical. The luxurious interior puts most hotel rooms into the shade – and you can change the view from your window as often as you like!

Hiring is the ideal way to start. From April to October, you can hire one of our vehicles from our base near Southampton (or we can meet you at Heathrow or Gatwick airports). You must be between 23 and 70, be acceptable for insurance and hold a full driving licence. We take a lot of time and trouble showing you how to drive it, and how everything works inside.

You can hire by the week, or, if you have longer expeditions in mind, you can use our 'buy-back' scheme – a really economical proposition if your trip's going to take weeks or even months. Ask for our brochure for all the details.

Your vehicle comes equipped with everything you need, including cutlery, crockery, gas, maps etc – jump in and go! Even linen is available, and is provided free for overseas customers. (And if you get hooked and decide to buy within a year, we'll deduct the price of a week's hire from the price of your vehicle – we're leaders in sales as well as hire).

We have three sizes of motor caravan on offer; a 5.25m four-berth, a 5.9m five-berth and a 7m six-berth. They're all less than a year old, and of superb quality.

Real explorers, look no further!"

EVERNDEN CYCLES

47 Maidstone Road, Paddock Wood, Kent TN12 6DG
Tel: 01892 832823. Fax: 01892 832931

"Go exploring by bike – or go exploring on four wheels, take your bike with you and use it to transform your holiday when you get there.

Any bike can be fitted with racks and panniers, so that you can carry a full camping outfit with you – there are even special tents available with built-in bike sheds!. Equally, bikes can be carried on most vehicles – on the roof, on the boot, on the tailgate or using a towbar rack. A caravan or motor caravan dealer will advise you.

Cycling is booming, with lots of people coming back to it who haven't cycled since schooldays. A wonderful choice of cycles is available, and prices are reasonable. Important, though, to choose the right type.

Kids are easy – mountain bikes are available everywhere, they're tough enough for the most enthusiastic rough-ground riding and they're fashionable. Adults may have, deep in the coalshed, an old 'town' bike. Best leave it there – these are too heavy for most country riding. Best ignore also the glamorous (drop handlebar) road tourers and racing bikes. Picture yourself leading the Tour de France if you will, but these thoroughbred mounts are expensive and a little fragile for careering around campsites.

The solution is the recently-developed, hybrid 'town and country' bike, hugely popular because it suits all purposes – we sell hundreds. It's a traditional large-wheeled bike with an upright riding position, yet much lighter than a town bike (which you'll appreciate when you're loading it onto a bike rack or carrying it across a stile!). With 18 or 21 gears, it has medium-width, rugged tyres, and is ideal for using round the town and for light off-road use – forest tracks, canal towpaths and the like. By far the best buy.

All sorts of accessories, special clothing (don't forget your helmet) and cycle route books exist now to make this a smashing leisure activity and one of the best ways imaginable of keeping fit. Much better than trudging over the Alps with elephants!"

Photos courtesy of Dawes Cycles Ltd.

Tourer Marketing Bureau

Brahm Building, Alma Road, Headingley, LEEDS LS6 2AH
Telephone: 0113 230 4000

'Hannibal should have got himself a touring caravan. Half a million Brits have, and it's the most popular form of holiday in Britain. Hook it up to your existing car (or elephant) and off you go. Arrive at your destination, unhook it and you've got your car to go wherever you will and your 'base' to return to – unbeatable flexibility.

It's not hugely expensive either. A very good second hand model with all mod cons – and they really are mod – can be bought for about £3,000 (and if you're on a tight budget you'll find older ones for much less than that). A brand new one will probably be between £8,000 and £20,000, depending on how big (and how glamorous) you want it to be.

And glamorous they certainly are – look at the 'interior' picture below. Hand-crafted furniture, interior sprung beds and superb upholstery make for a feeling of real luxury. Newcomers are often astonished to find central heating, hot water, showers, flush toilets, fridge-freezers and microwaves. Many people now use their caravans all the year round – if you enjoy being out and about whatever the weather, you have a really cosy home-from-home to use as a base.

Would-be touring caravan explorers should consider joining the Caravan Club, the Camping and Caravanning Club – or both. These two excellent organisations provide information on everything you need to know about caravanning.

A touring caravan opens up whole new worlds to you. Go away every weekend, take long holidays without worrying about hotel bills. Have a base for sports and hobbies. Discover a whole world of wonderful places.

Each year nearly seventy million holiday nights are spent in caravans. To find out everything you could possibly need to know about it all, give us a ring – we've got a smashing information pack available, absolutely free!

"Frankly, we at Autosleepers think Hannibal would have felt he'd missed out if he'd known about motor caravans. For expeditions large or small, they're ideal.

AUTOSLEEPERS LTD
Orchard Works
Willersey, nr Broadway
Worcestershire
WR12 7QF
England
Tel: 01386 853338
Fax: 01386 858343

The first huge advantage is that they can be whatever you want them to be. Your own grandstand for the races, a personal beach hut, an idyllic restaurant by the lake or just somewhere to take in the view. It's your personal life support machine, with room to relax, sleep, eat, wash and store your gear. And the second advantage is that they give you real 'get up and go' exploring. It's immediate – you're ready to hit the road whenever you decide to – for a day, a weekend, a holiday (or even crossing the Alps and invading other countries!)

There are two basic styles. The 'coachbuilt' is large and high, custom-built from the chassis up – a dedicated leisure vehicle. The 'high-top' is smaller, ideal for use as an everyday vehicle too, with an elevating roof to give you extra space when you stop. Either will accommodate two, three or four people in style.

And style it is too – one of the pleasures of choosing a motor caravan is discovering just how clever the interiors are. Tables, chairs, cupboards, lockers, wardrobes, beds, kitchens, even toilets and showers – room for everything you think you'll ever need, plus gas and electric appliances too. And perhaps the biggest surprise for the first-timer is the sheer quality and luxury of the fittings.

Autosleeper motor caravans are built onto specially-adapted base vehicles from Ford, Volkswagen, Peugeot, Renault and Mercedes. They are rugged and powerful, driving like cars and handling easily, even if you're a beginner. The cabs are superbly equipped and designed to be driver-friendly. Would-be buyers, as well as choosing their base vehicle, need to decide whether they prefer a petrol engine, a diesel or a turbo-diesel – each has its advantages. Autosleepers has a big choice of models, and all the experience needed to help you work out what's best for you. Pity we couldn't have told Hannibal!"

The VW Camper Centre

The VW Camper Centre – by junction 13 of the M25
Bell Weir Garage, Hythe End, Wraysbury, Berks TW19 6HE
Tel: 01784 483438/01753 542260 Fax: 01784 483303

The much-loved – and still very practical – Grand Daddy of all campers! For thousands and thousands of fans the world over, the ONLY way to go exploring. Own a VW and you have style; this is a real fun vehicle, and driving one makes you realise you're part of a club, as fellow owners wave to you as they pass and people stop to admire it nostalgically. And if you want to you can LITERALLY join a club – there are owner's clubs everywhere, rallies, magazines, shows ....!

But is it practical? It most certainly is. Buy one for something between £1,000 and £10,000; there are a million variations on the original 1950's 1131cc model. If you can't find just what you want, one can easily be altered, converted, upgraded or downgraded to suit. You can use it as an everyday vehicle; it's no longer than the average estate car. It's a sound investment too – resale values are always high.

For exploring, it's amazing. Stop, put the brake on and turn it into a home – quicker than a caravan. Use it as it is or raise the elevating roof and sleep four. Add an awning to the side and your living space is more than doubled. Internal fittings incorporate beds, cupboards, tables, seats, cookers, sinks – there are endless permutations. It's easy to drive, mechanically simple, robust and amazingly reliable, with parts easy to find all over Europe and beyond. More than Hannibal could say for his elephants!

Owning your own 'veedub' could be the fun way to low-cost camping for you, whether you want to take the odd weekend on the coast or to go off round the world (there aren't many places VW campers haven't been!). We have a unique deal on all our vehicles from the early 70s to the present day. Buy your vehicle, and off you go; finish your trip and we'll guarantee to buy it back from you – if you can bear to part with it! This can be an amazingly cheap way to take that trip of a lifetime.

Here at the VW Camper Centre we've dealt solely with these wonderful machines for over thirty years – growing up with them is an experience on its own. Come and have a look, and you'll see why!

Three good reasons why a real explorer should choose a tent!

Millets Leisure Limited
Mansard Close, Westgate, Northampton NN5 5DL
Tel: 01604 441111 Fax: 01604 441164

Firstly, tent camping offers you the best of both worlds. You can carry your home on your back and travel wherever you like without any ties, or you can take all the luxuries of home with you and 'live' in the great outdoors with all the luxuries you require. There are tents small enough to carry around with you, and there are others which can accommodate the largest family. We can supply a tent for any purpose, given over 155 stores (which also offer advice and back-up) – more than any other 'outdoor' retailer in the UK.

Tent camping can also be very cheap – we at Milletts like to think that camping can give you the freedom to explore the places you want to at a cost that is easily affordable. Quality tents can cost as little as £50. Equally, they can cost as much as £1,000 – it depends on what type of tent you want and what features it has. The important thing is to decide what you need from it. Consider questions such as:

- How many people will the tent sleep?
- Will it offer extra space for rucksack, boots etc?
- Does it need to be small and light enough to carry?
- Is it quick to put up in rainy weather?
- Does it have an inner tent? (Very cheap tents exist which look good value for money but don't have this important feature).

Another vital question – can the shop from which you bought it offer good after-sales service? Modern tents are tough, but they still need looking after – you need to be sure that you'll be able to replace say a flysheet or guyline for the model you've bought. When it comes to accessories, value for money is paramount, and this is where our expertise comes in. Are you going to use that sleeping bag once – in which case you don't need to spend £100 on it – or over and over again, in which case it might be a good investment? And what about cooking and eating equipment, tough yet light enough to carry? We've got it all!

Finally, tent camping is REAL camping – and quite simply, **FUN!**

Tourist Information to Enhance your Travels

The great explorers would have found discovering continents much easier if there'd been Tourist Information Centres. The British Isles have hundreds, each covering an individual town or local areas, and also has a network of Regional Tourist Boards. Each Regional Board can give you information on its whole area and can put you in touch with individual Information Centres too.

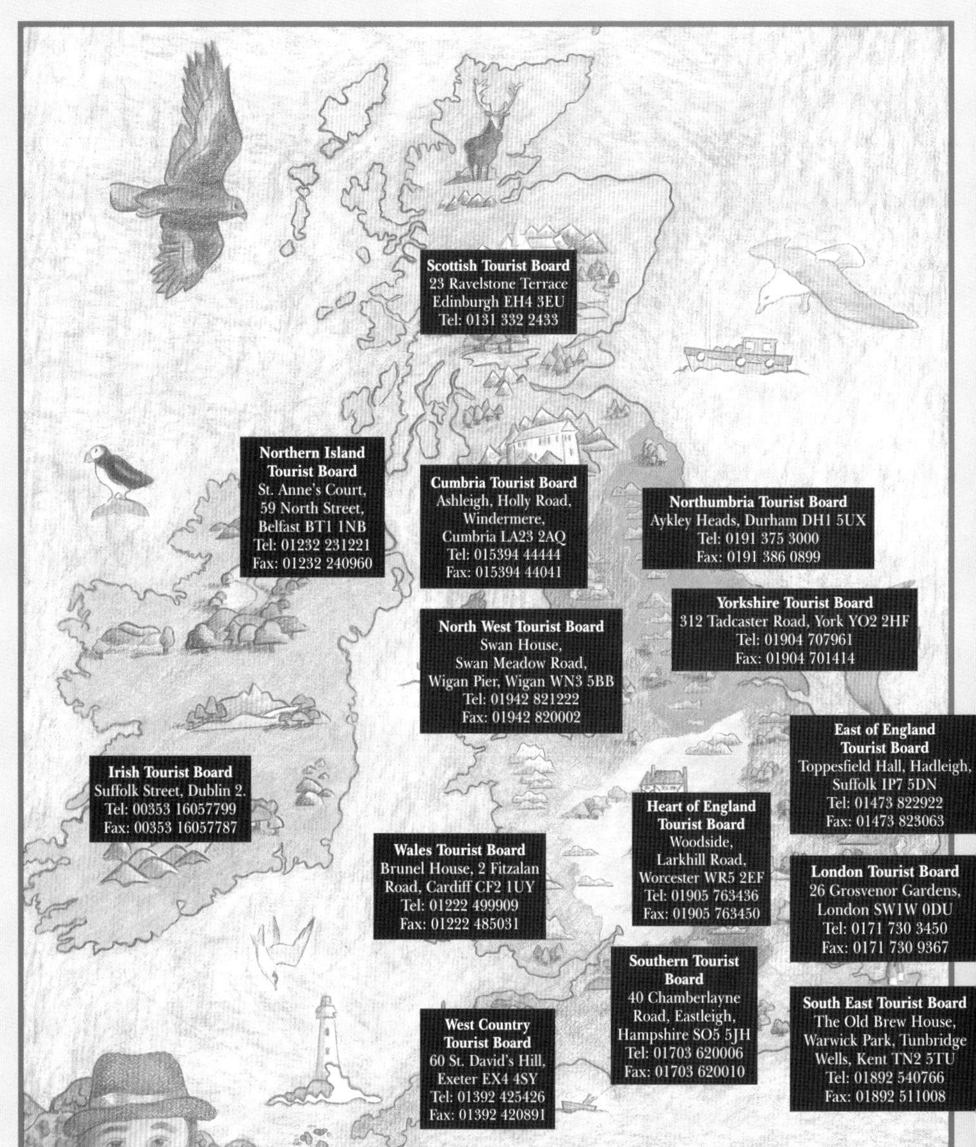

Food on the move is fun.
If you're reading this and picturing a microscopic caravan kitchen, no storage space and four mouths to feed three times a day, this may seem unlikely. If you're seeing yourself weighed down with a rucksack and struggling to heat beans on a stove with the output of a nightlight, this may seem certifiably deluded. But read on. The secret is contained in a few simple rules.
1. Pore over maps, not cookbooks. Empty your mind of usual habits – that's what holidays are about. Forget what you eat at home, when you eat it, where you shop for it, how you cook it. This is the time for something completely different
Eat when you feel like it, or when it fits in with your travels. Maybe you like to travel early, stop for a giant breakfast at eleven and then eat in the pub in the evening. Maybe the best part of your day is arriving at a site, opening the wine and settling down for a four-hour feast. Maybe you like to live on chocolate bars and those lukewarm beans. There are no rules. Be decadent and enjoy it.
2. Enjoy the hunting and gathering. Make shopping part of the fun – not a chore. Enjoy discovering fresh food along the way – free range eggs sold by the roadside, fruit and vegetables from farm shops, fish straight from the boats. Look out for the signs, buy when you spot them and concoct your next meal from whatever you've bought and whatever you can persuade yourself goes with it.
Look out for 'Pick Your Own' signs. (I do wonder how overseas visitors interpret this phrase, and others. 'No Cats Eyes For Three Miles', I saw the other day). Whatever it is, pick it. Catch your own fish, gather your own mushrooms and round up your own blackberries, if you're ambitious.
Forget your usual supermarkets – the routine trolley-trudge has nothing to do with holidays. Hunt down little shops in little villages, and interesting High Streets; try the butcher's peculiar game pie or the baker's homemade pizza. Go for that odd lumpy vegetable you've never tried. You can always play football with it. Shopping can be leisurely and interesting. It can mean meeting people, and chatting, and getting a feel for the character of a town or a village. And you don't have to be in Paris to sit in a cafe for an hour and watch the world go by.
Make a game of the regional specialities. Buy Cornish pasties in Cornwall and York ham in York; hardly a place is without some culinary oddity of its own. The buns of Britain alone would make a fortnight's trail.
3. Don't panic about nutrition. It takes more than a fortnight to die of scurvy. Man can live on canned food alone, or burnt sausages, or thrice-daily fish and chips, for the duration of a holiday. Grab and enjoy the wealth of fresh food these islands have to offer when you can, and when you can't, relish the novelty, the decadence, the frisson of wickedness that only true junk food can offer. You may miss out on the glow of virtue of creating three dietitian's dreams a day. But you'll avoid the life-shortening stress of shopping for them on the run and cooking them on a gas ring in a foot-square kitchen.
4. Never cook inside what you can cook out. Which means barbecues, the canny camper's best friend. Carry a big one if you will, or buy the tiny disposable ones. Don't let them sit them on the ground and burn the grass. Charcoal a chop, a fish or two or whatever takes your fancy. Drop it in the dirt a few times for real flavour. Add salad, cheese and fresh fruit. Manna from heaven.
Nearly (but not quite) everything can be barbecued, and it's fun experimenting. Discover who paid attention in the Scouts. Cook breakfast on it, warm up soup (in the opened can) on it, use it to heat up a concoction from the deli or to toast a cheese sandwich. Farewell to cooking in confined spaces and sleeping with the smells. No fuss about setting tables, less washing up. More outdoors.
Some ladies may have noticed that some gentlemen are really not all that 'new'. Forget the feminist arguments (or any arguments) about sharing the cooking. Men are drawn to barbecues like moths. Buy one, light and retire.
In some places, where there's space, fuel and no danger, you can still light camp fires. Don't miss these opportunities. There are few worse ways of cooking food, or better ones of restoring the soul.
5. Perfect your can-opening. Fun meals lurk in tins and packets you never buy. Store a few on board, have a few nifty recipes up your sleeve. Never worry again about finding somewhere to shop halfway up a mountain, twenty miles from a hamlet at ten past nine on a Sunday night.

The 'Real Exploring' Sites

WE'RE DELIGHTED to present to you 200 of the loveliest little corners of the British Isles for camping and caravanning – each one in the spirit of 'Real Exploring'. Mostly very small, very quiet and very simple, they are chosen for their position, their intrinsic interest and the absence of intrusive commercialisation.

- USE the centre map to see where the sites are – each one has a number.
- REFER to the pages which follow to find out about their character, their particular features and the area around them
- CHECK in the reference section at the back for details of specific facilities, directions etc.
- PHONE (at a reasonable time) to double-check that the site is open and has space. If a specific facility is important to you (a washing machine, for example, or access to a telephone), check that it's still available. Information given in good faith when this guide was compiled can easily be overtaken by events. If something you need isn't listed, ask the owner's advice.
  By definition, our sites don't provide ultra-lavish facilities – but friendliness, helpfulness and real interest in camping come as standard!

We're committed to real camping, real caravanning and real exploring. Let us know about your adventures, what you think of the sites, what you'd like to see – we'll send a free 'Real Exploring' sticker in exchange for your tales. And if you'd like to nominate a site YOU know for inclusion in next year's guide, we'd love to hear about that too.

1 *London's royal hunting forest. The Elms at High Beech.*

London at your fingertips! Camp within sight of the City, with free transport to the Underground station, and have a perfect base for a London visit or holiday – deep in the heart of a royal hunting forest! Endless attractions in London, and then for contrast beautiful Epping Forest to explore. Lovely walks; cycle hire on site too. Twenty-four hour access so that you can come and go as you please; ideally placed for east coast/ ports/motorways. Large traditional pub with food, barbecues and family facilities next door. A super-friendly site with an international clientele and a visitors' book full of compliments.

☎ **0181 508 3749/1000 (fax 0181 508 9414)**

2 *Fun camping for charity. Tent City, London.*

London camping for the young and young-at-heart! Tent City is cheap, irrepressibly cheerful and gives all its profits to charity. Not small (200 pitches), not quiet but surely deserving of inclusion in a guide to imaginative camping. About as close to London as you can get, the site has nevertheless a lovely canalside setting in the Lea Valley Nature Reserve; if you tire of the bright lights, explore the canalside pubs. All sorts of languages spoken; free practical help such as cooking facilities and baggage storage for wanderers from far and wide.

☎ **0181 985 7656 (fax 0181 749 9074)**

3 *Castles, coast and Sussex smugglers. Park Farm, Bodiam.*

Walk along the river to Bodiam Castle, fairytale castle owned by the National Trust and open to the public. Or walk for miles in gentle farmland - this site is in the heart of an Area of Outstanding Natural Beauty. Fish for free in the River Rother or light a camp fire; there's five acres here, so plenty of room for it. This is smugglers' country, where the gangs brought their spoils from the coast; a short drive takes you to picture-book Rye, or to Hastings with its fascinating Old Town. Discover the Cinque Ports; there were more than five, and some were inland.

☎ **01580 830514 (fax on same number)**

4

Pub camping in lovely Surrey.
'The Merry Harriers', nr. Godalming.

Camp in a lovely meadow and spend your evenings in the bar! This cosy old pub has an acre of land for campers in lovely surroundings midway between London and the coast. Footpaths and bridleways abound, and much of the surrounding countryside is carefully preserved by the National Trust. Inside, the Merry Harriers prides itself on being a Free House and on keeping its country pub character – bar food (lunchtime and evening) here, not restaurant meals! Inglenooks, beams, horse brasses and (apparently) chamberpots. More conventional loos provided too!

☎ **01428 682883** OPEN ALL YEAR

5

South Downs – history, scenery and coast.
The Old Mill, Golden Cross.

Sussex loves visitors, though perhaps the 1066 season brought some they'd have thought twice about. William did battle at Battle nearby, smugglers frequented Alfriston with its picture-postcard looks. A giant carved in a chalk hillside looks as if he's seen it all and more. Walk the Seven Sisters cliffs past Beachy Head, discover the castles and the little villages folded in the hills; this lovely downland country is rich in history and endowed with spectacular beauty. Enjoy it from this little site at Golden Cross, small but perfectly placed for exploring by vehicle or on foot.

☎ **01825 872532**

6

Traditional camping and traditional craftsmanship in Sussex.
Harwoods Farm, Henfield.

Mr Spear, master craftsman, has run his site for thirty two of his seventy five years. Some of 'his' families have been back every year since the beginning. This is timeless camping; simply a field by a river (tidal here, with fishing) with minimal facilities; miles of secluded footpaths close by and the south coast not much further. Vegetables and eggs can be bought from nearby farms; as for Mr Spear's award-winning wooden bowls, platters and goblets, the waiting list is two years long. Catch him when he's not too busy, though, and he'll be happy to show you how they're made.

☎ **01273 492820**

7 *Pints and evocative landscapes. The Cock Horse Inn, Peasmarsh.*

View from the beer garden! Pub camping is a real pleasure; a cosy refuge for the evenings, meals, snacks and drinks to hand and no driving to worry about. The Cock Horse Inn is near Rye, in the atmospheric Romney Marsh; explore the smugglers' villages (maybe by bike; it's gloriously flat). Winchelsea is close and pretty; Dungeness is further, bleak and dramatic, a strange landscape well worth an expedition with a free guided trip round the looming nuclear power station. Come back and argue the pros and cons of it all in the bar!

☎ **01797 230281**

8 *Idyllic farm camping on Kent/Sussex border. Manor Court Farm, Tunbridge Wells.*

Find your own little corner of paradise on this 350-acre sheep/arable farm with its pond (rowing boat) orchard and lovely old buildings. On high ground, the views are lovely all around, with abundant footpaths including the long-distance Wealdway and the Sussex Border Path. Sheep and ponies will keep an eye on you; cats, dogs and Louise (3) may drop in. Cream teas available, and B&B. Take the waters at nearby Tunbridge Wells, visit Churchill's home at Chartwell and Anne Boleyn's castle at Hever – much more too, by car, bike, bus or nearby train.

☎ **01892 740279**

9 *Gone fishing, one way or another. Brakes Coppice, near Hastings.*

A smashing spot only five miles from the coast, set in thirteen acres of glorious woodland with walks and paths. Brakes Coppice is secluded and peaceful, with room for kids to let off steam and have country adventures a-plenty. Its own coarse fishing lake too, for enjoying the peace while they're gone; if you don't catch anything edible, sneak off to nearby Hastings Old Town where the fishing boats are pulled right up onto the beach and fresh fish stalls abound. William the Conqueror wouldn't have bothered with London if he'd known about the fish and chip shops there.

☎ **01424 830322 (phone and fax)**

10

Rural life centre on edge of Ashdown Forest.
Heaven Farm, near Uckfield,Sussex.

Bluebell walks, nature trails, a fascinating farm museum, tea rooms, tours and a craft shop, within a mile of the famous Bluebell Railway and Sheffield Park Gardens. A lovely place to camp, with much to see and do. Beautiful woodland and waterside walks – not for nothing is the steam railway named after the bluebells, and the cool glades of foxgloves and drifts of snow-white anenomes are unforgettable. Launch an 'expotition' from here into Ashdown Forest, where Winnie the Pooh and his friends played; discover the sites of their adventures and rediscover the magic of childhood. Heaven indeed.

☎ 01825 790226, fax 01825 790881 OPEN ALL YEAR

11

Lovely valley in historic 1066 country.
Whydown Farm, near Battle, East Sussex.

A lovely farm site just down the road from Battle where the Normans beat the natives in 1066 – you can wander round the site and learn all about it. The surrounding countryside is much more peaceful – the site sits in the secluded, sun-trap Whydown Valley, and is as pretty as a picture. Nor far from the coast – try sea angling from Dungeness beach or Hastings pier. This is wine country too, where you can tour the vineyards, sample the wines and buy them to take away (wine was made in southern England LONG before the French arrived!). A perfect exploring base, handy for the ports.

☎ 01424 870147

12

Sussex exploring on foot or wheels.
Peel House Farm, Polegate, East Sussex.

Doves in the dovecote and the Cuckoo Trail on the doorstep – a path leads from this tranquil little rural site straight onto the Trail, a much-acclaimed walking/cycling path recently created from a railway track to make exploring Sussex on two wheels or two feet safe and pleasant. And this is country worth exploring – picturesque old villages and pubs, National Trust houses, market towns and seaside resorts and down the road lovely Drusilla's Zoo. Open views from the site – explore the South Downs (try the Southdowns Way path) and find seven sisters. An oasis of peace, near the port of Newhaven.

☎ 01323 845629

13 *Cider making and much else on country estate. Horam Manor, near Heathfield, East Sussex.*

The Horam Manor estate houses Merrydown Cider and Wines (tours and shop), a farm museum, a blacksmith's shop, horse riding, five fishing lakes, nature trails, a cafe and craft workshops – yet it still feels friendly, homely and very relaxed. Plenty to do if you want to – peace and tranquility if you don't. Camp in the seven acres of gently sloping grassland surrounded by beautiful wooded countryside in the Sussex Weald, an area of outstanding natural beauty. Nearby on the coast is Eastbourne, and not much further is Brighton, famous and fun.

☎ 01435 813662

14 *Pub camping for exploring coast and country. 'The Limeburners', near Billingshurst, West Sussex.*

Traditional country pub with camping. The building dates from the sixteenth century, and was once three thatched cottages housing families whose menfolk worked the adjacent lime kilns. Now it's a lovely inn serving food every day and providing explorers with a very civilised base. Close to the river Arun, which wends its way down to interesting Arundel, and close too to the National Trust's splendid Petworth House, open to the public (superb deer park). Older houses still – a Roman villa to see at Bignor and the famous Roman palace at Fishbourne if you follow the road to the sea. Super site for exploring all of West Sussex, coastal and inland.

☎ 01403 782311

15 *Way off the beaten track near Pooh country. St. Ives, Hartfield, Kent/Sussex border.*

An idyllic little spot on the northern edge of the Ashdown Forest. A small farm site with a lake; lots of people come coarse fishing here. Not far away is Poohsticks Bridge, where Winnie invented his famous game – you can go there and play it for yourself. Find out more in nearby Hartfield, which has a shop/tearooms totally dedicated to the famous bear of very little brain (but immortal charm), or wander into the forest and find the Visitor's Centre. Perfect country for explorers, and a landscape like no other in southern England. Unbelievably, once the iron-making centre of the country.

☎ 01892 770213

16 *Kent, coast and Canterbury.*
'Red Lion', Dunkirk.

People plan an overnight stop here because it's perfectly placed near Canterbury on the road to London. Then they realise just what they're missing by moving on, and come back for a whole holiday. A little site, surrounded by woodland, in beautiful, bird-filled countryside on the pilgrims' route to Canterbury. Next to a pub, with a farm shop opposite – not for nothing is Kent called the 'garden of England'. Four miles from Canterbury, five miles from the beaches and twenty minutes from ferries and Tunnel. Lovely landscapes and picture-book villages all around.

☎ 01227 750661 

17 *Seaside fun from a quiet corner.*
Pine Meadow, near Ramsgate, Kent.

Marmite the cat introduces himself to campers here as a rule, when he's not harrassing the peacocks – this is a lovely tucked-away little site in the grounds of a Georgian country mansion on a 350-acre arable farm. Set in an old meadow with lovely trees, flowers, partridges (and the long-suffering peacocks), it's quiet and pretty. Astonishingly, just down the road are the resorts of Broadstairs, Margate and Ramsgate, with all the fun and bustle of the seaside – enjoy it all, then retreat to this rare haven of tranquility on this busy Isle of Thanet. Golf centre nearby, and the adjacent village of Manston houses the Spitfire museum, a fascinating insight into aviation and the Battle of Britain.

☎ 01843 587770

18 *History and country calm en route to London.*
'To the Woods', West Kingsdown, Kent.

'To the Woods' is the name of this site, and to the woods you can certainly go – climb up from the farmer's field and walk to lovely Otford and Eynsford. Walk any other way you like too, and you'll find lovely North Downs countryside and olde worlde villages. An excellent little family site very well placed on the A20 going into London. Lots of famous folk lived near here; spectacular Knowle House at nearby Sevenoaks was home to Vita Sackville-West, Winston Churchill lived at Chartwell and General Wolfe at Westerham. A good area for lovers of fine houses and history.

☎ 01322 863751 (fax on same number) 

19 *England's enchanted island.*
Grange Farm, Brighstone, Isle of Wight.

Superfluous, given the picture, to tell you that this site is in an Area of Outstanding Natural Beauty. This is its own beach; you can walk for miles along golden sands and hunt for fossils, frequently found here, and swim safely and peacefully. On the farm, you'll find llamas and pot-bellied pigs plus a veritable Noah's Ark of other creatures great and small. Opposite the farm gate a restaurant offers bars, meals and takeaways, and picture-book, charming Brighstone is half a mile away. All this on the glorious Isle of Wight.

☎ **01983 740296**

20 *Horses at Cowes.*
Comforts Farm, Isle of Wight.

Next to the world-famous yachting centre of Cowes for lovers of messing about in boats, this riding school, with acres of woodland rides and its own pure Arabian stud, is paradise for lovers of horses too. And for lovers of wildlife - the camp site alone hosts fifty different wild flowers, with foxes, badgers, red squirrels and rare butterflies all around. Just along the coast is excellent sea fishing from the shore. Pop over from the mainland on foot or with a bike; the site's no distance from the ferry terminal. By car, everywhere on the island's reachable in half an hour.

☎ **01983 293888**

21 *Grounds of Hampshire private estate.*
The Spinney, Alresford.

The hidden treasure of Hampshire is its enchanting towns and villages - this is Alresford, one of the best of them. Timeless England; little shops and cafes, picture-book houses and soothing riverside walks. Camp close to it in the lovely, landscaped grounds of a private estate. Hinton Ampner, a fine National Trust house open to the public, is just up the road, and there are a great many other local attractions, including a famous steam railway. In days gone by, nearby Winchester was England's capital; its cathedral is stunning.

☎ **01962 732829**

22 *Cornfields, cycling and pretty villages. Brocklands Farm, near Petersfield.*

Wake up to the mist lifting off cornfields in this idyllic little corner of Hampshire. This friendly arable farm has lovely walks across the fields and a wonderful cycle route right next to it - a long, completely safe stretch of atmospheric, tree-shaded railway track with useful hostelries. West Meon village is picture-book pretty, as is so much of this county; Portsmouth, Winchester and the New Forest are not far.

☎ 01730 829446

23 *Forestry Commision camping in the New Forest. Longbeech, near Cadnam.*

One of two Forestry Commission sites in the New Forest left 'undeveloped' for back-to-nature camping. Longbeech is set in ancient beech woodland; camp in clearings between the trees and enjoy the tranquility and the animals (birds, squirrels, rabbits and LOTS of ponies). Walk into the forest; find an excellent pub and a stone marking William Rufus' downfall. Cycle paths here too - and lots of peace, quiet and wonderful woodland air.

☎ 01703 283771 (all Forestry Commission New Forest sites)

24 *Forestry Commission camping in the New Forest. Denny Wood, near Lyndhurst.*

A second Forestry Commission site, this time further south. Unspoilt natural surroundings - open grassland with scattered oak trees, where you can roam for miles and simply relish the peace. Ponies here too, meandering aimlessly and happy to be admired. This 'New' forest, by the way, is a thousand years old - William the Conqueror planted it as a base for a spot of hunting. Wild deer browse, and commoners' animals graze, much as they did then.

☎ 01703 283771
(all Forestry Commission New Forest sites)

25 ***Perfect for Dorset, Poole and the ferry.***
Huntick Farm, Lytchett Matravers.

A lovely little site perfect for exploring the South Coast and all its treaures and attractions. Sea and sand six miles away; the romantic Isle of Purbeck, scenic Hardy Country, gardens, great houses, resorts and museums to explore and enjoy. A tranquil rural setting near the pretty Dorset village of Lytchett Matravers. And if you're still determined to leave all this and take the Poole ferry out of the country, this is the perfect overnight stop for it.

☎ 01202 622222

26 ***Dorset coast – islands, bays and wildlife.***
Haycrafts, near Swanage.

Warmest of welcomes here at this superb little family site set in beautiful rolling countryside. Oliver Cromwell wrecked dramatic Corfe Castle nearby, which only seems to have made it more popular than ever – the lovely village nestling at its feet bustles with visitors, and provided the set for 'The Mayor of Casterbridge'. The coastal walks and beaches are truly spectacular; cross the bay to the National Trust's Brownsea Island, where the beleaguered red squirrel, ousted from the mainland by his American cousins, takes refuge.

☎ 01929 480572

27 ***Fascinating coast and fascinating countryside.***
Haddons Farm, near Wimborne.

A lovely, secluded farm campsite, on the edge of seven hundred acres of glorious country park (which offers, intriguingly, tree top walks) and the Purbeck hills. Bournemouth, Poole, the sea and the coast are close – but look inland too. There you'll find the New Forest, Georgian towns, splendid Salisbury with its soaring cathedral and fine National Trust houses. Truly a region which will keep you occupied for a month, and a tranquil little base from which to enjoy it.

☎ 01202 822582

28 *Odd creatures and easy access to London. Highclere Farm, Beaconsfield.*

The gentleman with the amazing ears is a pedigree Anglo-Nubian goat; his woolly friends are pets on this working farm, which produces among other things wonderful free range eggs for sale in the farm shop. Other odd animals live at the Rare Breeds Centre down the road, and shire horses too. This is a perfect base for touring pretty Buckinghamshire, and for London too – half an hour by train from the station in the village. Lots of family pubs with facilities for kids – six within three miles.

☎ 01494 874505, fax 01494 875238

29 *Near main routes and away from it all. Oakley Farm, Newbury.*

Canal boats chug through Newbury; canal tow paths make wonderful walks, especially in areas as pretty as this. Larger boats come and go from the ferry port at Southampton, an hour away, and the M4 is only three miles away. If you're looking for a stopover site, this is one where you'll want to stop for longer. Oakley Farm is pretty and friendly, with lovely lanes all around. From here you could visit the Queen at Buckingham Palace OR at Windsor Castle.

☎ 01635 36581

30 *Picture-book villages and famous places. Mollington Park, near Banbury.*

Mollington is the sort of village that finds itself on the lids of chocolate boxes. Wander through lovely gardens from the site and find yourself at the village pub; there are pleasant strolls in all directions. Strike out further and find yourself in some of England's most famous places. Stratford-on-Avon is not far, nor are Oxford and Warwick. The Cotswolds, full of beautiful houses like this, is all around you.

☎ 01295 750731

31 *Idyllic and immortalised.*
Bridge House, Clifton Hampden.

"Round Clifton Hampden, itself a wonderfully pretty village, old-fashioned, peaceful and dainty with flowers, the river scenery is rich and beautiful". So said Jerome K Jerome, whose 'three men in a boat' did a great deal of messing about on the river round here, fishing and visiting local hostelries; no finer place than this site to follow their excellent example. Private stretch of Thames for fishing, moorings etc. All this and London only an hour away, Oxford's dreaming spires 10 miles.

☎ **01865 407725**

32 *Oxford base on edge of Cotswolds.*
Diamond Farm, Bletchington.

On the edge of the Cotswolds. This is essence of England, a world of golden stone, picture-postcard villages and landscapes to make your heart lift. Leave the A34 or the M40 and within minutes you're at friendly Diamond Farm, from where you can tour it all and the Chiltern Hills too. Horseriding close by. A perfect spot for exploring Oxford.

☎ **01869 350909, fax 01869 350918** OPEN ALL YEAR

33 *Boat hire base on the Thames.*
Benson Pleasurecraft, near Wallingford.

Benson Pleasurecraft welcome campers at their boat hire base on the beautiful Thames just south of Oxford. Cruiser bases like this are fascinating places to sit and watch the world go by; they have day boats for hire and fishing permits too. Boats and pubs go hand in hand, and a ten-minute walk takes you to the village with a choice of hostelries. Tour the Cotswolds and the Thames valley from here by land, or take to the river and tour it afloat.

☎ **01491 838304 (phone/fax)**

34 *Bashful pub worth searching for. 'The White Horse Inn', Priors Dean, Hampshire.*

Half the fun of camping here is finding the place. Known as 'the pub with no name', for reasons which are clear from the picture, this modestly anonymous establishment is buried deep in it's own twelve acres of land deep in the Hampshire countryside. A real find, though – rural, peaceful and away from traffic, for simple, countryside camping. The pub prides itself on its ten cask-conditioned ales and its lack of ostentation and over-commercialisation. It prides itself too on its food, all prepared by landlady Sue, who's a chef.

☎ **01420 588387**

35 *Parkland camping on the Duke of Wellington's estate. Wellington Country Park, near Reading, Berks.*

The Duke of Wellington's estate extends over 350 acres of beautiful wooded parkland and encompasses a lovely little camping and caravanning site. Here you can walk for miles in the woods, go boating on the lake or coarse fishing, eat in the cafeteria and indulge yourself in the gift shop; lots for children to see and do too. Leave this lovely country park and you'll find you're well placed for touring – London, Windsor, Salisbury, Winchester and Oxford are all within easy reach. Camp here in wonderful surroundings and be totally, utterly spoilt for choice.

☎ **01189 326444, fax 01189 326445**

36 *Travellers' rest – explorers' base. Hillcrest, Whiteparish.*

Perfectly placed for touring, just off the A36 Bristol-Southampton road. Stop off for a night and you'll find more places to visit from here than you'll manage in a month – the New Forest, Thomas Hardy's Wessex, Stonehenge, Exbury Gardens, Beaulieu, Winchester and the South Coast. Portsmouth with its famous collection of historic ships (and more modern ones going to France and the Isle of Wight) is close. Golf and horse riding not far from the site; nearby Whiteparish can be reached on foot and has all you need. Friendly, comfortable, secluded and open all year.

OPEN ALL YEAR

☎ **01794 884471**

37 *In the steps of the Druids. Stonehenge Touring Park.*

Druids have danced round Stonehenge for a thousand years (not the same ones). Mysterious and majestic, it sits on dramatic Salisbury Plain and exudes timelessness. Traces – and the atmosphere- of prehistory are everywhere; the vistas are open and dramatic and wildlife abounds on this undulating plateau. Experience it from this pretty site adjoining the friendly village shop and Post Office in ancient Orcheston (mentioned in the 11th century Domesday Book – positively modern in this part of the world!). The shop has all you need, including Off Licence and camping gas. Wonderful cooked breakfasts available. Internationally renowned, and justifiably.

☎ **01980 620304, fax 01980 621121**

38 *Forest, plain, coast and cathedral cities. Alderbury, Salisbury*

This new site is cheery, friendly and conveniently opposite a pub which serves food. It's also within three miles of Salisbury, a lovely market town built on no less than five rivers with the tallest cathedral spire in the country. The elegant cathedral close has fine buildings and museums; nearby Wilton House is open to the public in the summer. A smashing little base for exploring the New Forest, Salisbury Plain and the south coast. Country walks and good cycling country all around, with fishing too.

☎ **01722 710125** OPEN ALL YEAR

39 *At the foot of a famous flight. Lower Foxhangers Farm, near Devizes.*

The Kennet and Avon canal, recently restored, has many locks on its route from west of London to Bristol and Bath. Twenty-nine of them form a spectacular staircase here, one of the great monuments and meeting points of the English canal network. Watch the peculiar long, thin boats go by, or if you're feeling charitable help their crews work all those lock gates! The canal teems with fish, especially carp, with frequent monster catches of 10-20lbs. The farm sells fishing permits, and has canoes and dinghies for hire too. Walk along the towpath here and discover the best route to Devizes devised.

☎ **01380 828795, fax 01380 828254**

40 *Somerset, ancient and alcoholic.*
Thorney Lakes, Somerset Levels.

Camp in a cider orchard. Explore this conservation-award-winning farm in the atmospheric, timeless landscape of the Somerset Levels. Fish in Thorney Lakes (giant carp) or roam the wetlands with their wealth of flora, fauna and birdlife. Down the road the historic village of Muchelney is positively bursting with discoveries; its ancient Abbey, its Priest House (National Trust), church, gardens, pottery ... you'll positively burst, too, if you try all the local delicacies to be found near here. Pick your own fruit and vegetables, taste a cornucopia of delicacies from the Smokery and wash it all down with cider and cider brandy.

☎ **01458 250811**

41 *Lovely pub in lovely surroundings.*
Lowtrow Cross Inn, nr. Taunton

Ancient and cheery pub with local ales, bar meals, pool, darts and skittles and beer garden – plus its own camping area in acres of unspoilt countryside. On the edge of Exmoor, this is paradise for walkers, cyclists and car tourers; you can ride and fish here too, and if you catch anything the owners will freeze it for you. Takeaway food, B&B and the Great British Sunday Lunch all available. If you can drag yourselves away from all this, there are all manner of smashing days out to be had. Mr Blobby lives down the road.

☎ **01398 371111/371220**

42 *A little patch of paradise.*
Southdown Farm, near Brixham.

The most beautiful breakfast view in Devon – and a rare, rare oasis of tranquility on this famous coast. Sheep and horses share the field; neighbours are few and literally far between. A few minutes' walk takes you onto the stunning South Coast Footpath and, believe it or not, the hustle and bustle of Brixham is only a mile away. Only three or four pitches, so ring in advance, and check the directions too, especially if you're towing. The picture paints a thousand words. A gem.

☎ **01803 857991 (phone and fax)**

43 *Essence of Dartmoor. Ashburton.*

Hidden in a sheltered, south-facing valley in the beautiful Dartmoor National Park is this oasis of tranquility. Woods border this prettiest of sites, which adjoins the open moor, and the shallow river Ashburn with its rocky pools babbles through it. Walk, ride, fish, climb or even letter-box (a verb, it seems; ask the owners!). Dartmoor is glorious. The coast is not far, and there are dozens of attractions nearby. A gentle walk takes you to Ashburton, a stannary town. Discover the meaning of this word too, and with it much of the fascinating history of this region.

☎ **01364 652552**

44 *Relaxation on the rocks. Bundu, near Okehampton.*

A small, relaxed and quiet site, although, say the owners, the chink of glasses is acceptable. Put your glasses down long enough to do some exploring, and you'll find you're perfectly placed here, half a mile from the main A30. Drive across Dartmoor and discover oddly-named beauty spots, dramatic gorges and an even more dramatic prison. Plymouth and the Devonport naval dockyard are not far either, for original expeditions. Or you could simply sit back, revel in the scenery and open another bottle.

☎ **01837 861611**

45 *Warmest of Devon welcomes, just off the A30. Barley Meadow, near Exeter.*

Freedom, friendship and fun – the motto of this lovely Devon site, where even the dogs are friendly. Warm and welcoming Devon is a feast for the senses; here are flowers a-plenty, picture-book villages and the legendary cream tea (doctors and health food fanatics avert your eyes). A restaurant next door too in case you haven't quite indulged yourself enough. And all around you the National Park and scenery like this, Fingle Bridge across the river Teign.

☎ **01647 281629**

46 *At the estuary mouth.*
Yeate Farm, Bodinnick-by-Fowey.

A small, friendly family farm, in a glorious spot right on the Fowey estuary. Bring a boat and launch it from the slipway, or simply sit and watch the boats go by – the Old Ferry Inn is conducive to this time-honoured activity. Fishing is good in the river, and inland there are lakes and reservoirs on Bodmin Moor. Walkers will revel in the surrounding countryside, much of which is in the care of the National Trust.

☎ **01726 870256**

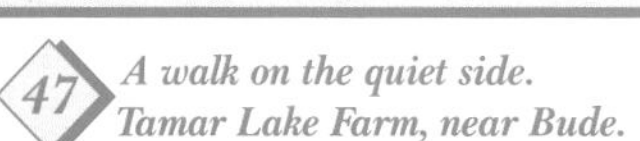

47 *A walk on the quiet side.*
Tamar Lake Farm, near Bude.

Explore Cornwall's north coast – rugged, scenic and largely unspoilt. From this rural haven you can walk to nearby Tamar Lakes, where there are birds to watch, fish to catch and a certain amount of messing about in (quiet) boats to be done; there are riding stables, and lovely open countryside for walks. Or follow the famous coastal path. Not far from a pretty village, and not far either from Sandy Mouth beach, from where you can walk along five miles of sand into Bude. Only when the tide's out, though – take care.

☎ **01288 321426**

48 *Much to do, or do nothing.*
Trevean Farm, near Padstow.

A lovely farm site for enjoying spectacular north Cornwall. Activities for the energetic include coastal walks, horse riding, pony trekking, surfing, wind surfing, swimming, sailing, fishing and golf. Activities for the energetically challenged include exploring the pretty village of St Merryn (shops, cafe and four pubs) and discovering the many good eateries nearby. And watching the world go by in the lovely little port of Padstow, four miles away.

☎ **01841 520772**

49

Picture-book village near Chesil Beach.
Home Farm, Puncknowle, Dorset.

Just inland from magnificent Chesil Beach; you can walk it for miles. Follow the coastal path and maybe go all the way to Weymouth (paradise for seafood lovers). This is the Heritage Coast, with coves and castles and spectacular views whichever way you look. The little site at Home Farm has lovely views too; the village is picturesque and includes a sixteenth century thatched pub which serves excellent food. Explorers may quickly discover a swannery and some sub-tropical gardens – it could take you a month to unearth all that is to be found near here.

☎ **01308 897258**

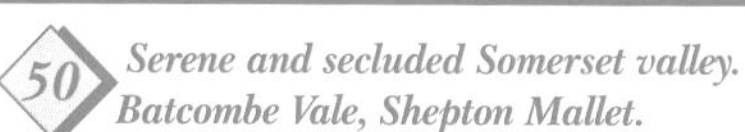

50

Serene and secluded Somerset valley.
Batcombe Vale, Shepton Mallet.

Share this site with rabbits, buzzards and heron; be deafened by the plop of the fish, the munching of the cows and the incessant song of the blackbirds. Potter around in a rowing boat, and hide away with a book in a shady glade; fish, or spot the birds, flowers and butterflies. A dream environment, an enclosure of trees, lakes and wild landscaped gardens around Batcombe Vale House, deep in an area of outstanding natural beauty. Wander the Green Hills of Somerset (lots of circular walks) and if you can bear to, venture further afield and discover attractions and outings galore. A lovely little site in a wonderful setting.

☎ **01749 830246 EMail: 100421.3001@compuserve.com**

51

Hills, gorges, caves, legends and cheese.
Mendip Heights, near Wells, Somerset.

A fascinating spot, in the heart of the Mendip Hills, surrounded by caves, gorges and legends. Tour the caverns at Cheddar where earliest man lived in eerie and fantastic surroundings, or find out what's at the bottom of Wookey Hole. Visit mystical Glastonbury with its ancient legends, and ancient Priddy too, just up the road with legends of its own. Wander through the beautiful valley of Ebbor Gorge, looked after by the National Trust. Discover England's smallest city and the world's best cheese. This is a real country site, where the proprietors are totally committed to outdoor-life camping – ask them about canoeing, abseiling, mountain biking, archery, caving and free guided walks with Mendip Rangers.

☎ **01749 870241**

52 *Quiet farm base for exploring beautiful Clovelly*
Dyke Green Farm, Clovelly, Devon.

'It is as if the place had stood still while all the world had been rushing and rumbling past it.' Thus said Charles Kingsley, who lived here in Clovelly while his father was curate at the church. Water babies will love it – everybody loves it. Beat the crowds – enjoy the hustle and bustle of one of the world's prettiest and most visited villages from the tranquil little camp site at Dyke Green Farm. Enjoy the coastal walks too from here. The farmhouse supplies produce from two local farms – delivered twice a day in season, so it really IS fresh.

☎ 01237 431699 Fax 01237 431689

53 *Monks' fishery for exploring Devon and beyond.*
Fishponds House, near Honiton, Devon.

The carp keeper of Dunkerswell Abbey lived in the cottage which grew into Fishponds House – it was built in 1201, when the Abbey was founded. The monks raised carp for food; of their thirty-one original ponds, four remain and are in these grounds. Set in the stunning Blackdown Hills at the head of the beautiful river Otter, which flows out to sea at Budleigh Salterton, this is a tiny and interesting site from which the whole of Devon, the west Dorset coast and the Somerset coast can easily be reached. Coarse fishing, of course – they've been doing that for about eight hundred years here!

☎ 01404 891358 Fax 01404 891109

54 *Lovely little conservation award site in pretty valley.*
Carbeil, near Looe, Cornwall.

This lovely little twenty-pitch site has won an award from the David Bellamy Conservation Foundation for its excellent work in preserving the wildlife and plants which share its lovely little patch of Cornwall. Bats, owls, squirrel and pheasant abound, and the unspoilt banks host wild flowers common and rare. Set in a pretty valley ten minutes from the sea, this is the place to stay to enjoy all the delights of Looe and the coast without the commercialisation; a neat and friendly little haven of natural camping in a spectacular part of the West Country.

☎ 01503 250636

55 *Perfect country camping in heart of Cornwall. Ruthern Valley, near Bodmin.*

Squirrels tapping on your windows for food, and forty different types of birds squabbling for scraps – this is outdoor life camping par excellence. Space for games, woods and tree-ropes to give kids hours of happy, healthy play, yet so much space that there's peace and quiet for everyone. From here you can walk or cycle the traffic-free and blessedly flat Camel Trail (named after the river, not the less-than-flat animal) into the famous north coast fishing port of Padstow. Or follow the 'Pilgrim's Route' incorporating many lovely churches from there to Fowey on the south coast. Eggs, clotted cream, Cornish Scrumpy and of course Cornish Pasties on site.

☎ 01208 831395, or freephone 0500 15 16 10

56 *Super little site in westernmost Cornwall. Bosavern House, St. Just.*

Explore the harbours and coves of western Cornwall, all the way down to Land's End, from this winner of a site in the lovely old walled garden of a country house (B&B too). Wonderful hospitality and every assistance in making the most of the enormous amount there is to see and do here. An 'Area of Outstanding Natural Beauty', a 'Heritage Coast' AND an 'Area of Great Historic Interest'! One hundred major archeological sites, coastal flights from Land's End airport, the Minack Open Air Theatre, surfing at Sennen Cove and much, much more. Walk across three fields to the town of St. Just, with all you need.

☎ 01736 788301

57 *Flower farm on a tiny island paradise. Troytown Farm, Scilly Isles.*

St Agnes, Scilly Isles, is a mile across, traffic free and truly, intoxicatingly beautiful. Camp here on a flower farm, where early narcissi are grown throughout the winter. There are dramatic bays and white sandy beaches, clear water perfect for diving and snorkelling and clear skies free of pollution where the stars sparkle. From the site you can see Bishop Rock Lighthouse and watch the sunset from your tent door. No cars (and alas no caravans/motor caravans) on the island- a tractor takes your luggage to the site. Trailer tents OK. Phone for details of availability, and of how to get to this island paradise. The camping experience of a lifetime.

☎ 01720 422360

58 *Tiny farm site in lovely Colne valley.*
Seven Arches Farm, near Colchester, Essex.

Set among the meadows of the lovely Colne Valley on the Essex/Suffolk border, a tiny site on a hundred-acre arable and sheep farm (B&B too). Handy for Harwich and Felixstowe but well away from the noisy A12, this is a lovely base for enjoying the landscapes immortalised by Constable and Gainsborough – you can go and find them from here. Lavenham, Kersey, Clare and Cavendish make up an excellent tour of Suffolk villages, and if you're feeling extravagant try Coggeshall with its twelve antique shops. If you're not, the views, the tranquility and the riverside walks are absolutely free.

☎ **01206 574896**

59 *Useful stop for East Anglian travellers.*
Grange Farm, Downham Market, Norfolk.

A useful little site off the A134 between Colchester and King's Lynn, very convenient for east coast ports. Stretch your legs with a good cycle ride, or unwind with a bit of fishing in the river. There's a National Trust property to investigate two miles away, and the traditional market towns of Swaffham and Downham Market are not far either. Don't be in too much of a hurry to bypass Colchester, once a major Roman garrison town, or King's Lynn, an old Hanseatic port.

☎ **01366 500307**

60 *Fens, flowers, walks and wildfowl.*
Matapos, near Hargate, Lincs.

Flowers, flowers and more flowers – the Fens are a gardener's delight, especially in May when Spalding has its famous Festival. Whatever the time of year, their are nurseries a-plenty round here, with all sorts of shows and special events. This is a lovely little site to use as a base for exploring it all, or maybe visiting nearby Sandringham; it's also well-placed if you're travelling up to Yorkshire. Lovely walks – you can follow in the footsteps of bishops, or walk out from the former lighthouse home of Sir Peter Scott along the seabanks of the wash. Excellent cycling too, and more pretty towns, attractions and places to visit than you'd ever have imagined.

☎ **01406 422910**

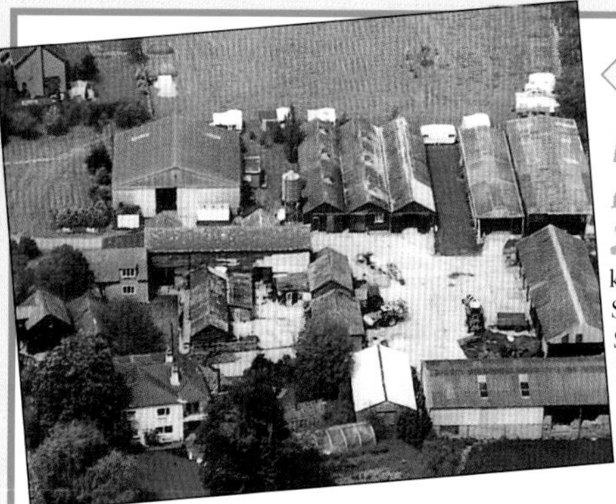

61 *Warm farm welcome in historic Suffolk.*
Brighthouse Farm, near Bury St Edmunds.

Perfect Suffolk touring base, between picture-book Long Melford and historic Bury St Edmunds, in countryside to set Constable drooling. A happy, friendly working farm where the welcome (and farmer John's cooked breakfasts) are second to none and the guests keep coming back. Farm trail to explore; B&B available. Smashing pub with wonderful food nearby. Fascinating Bury St Edmunds gave birth to Magna Carta – visit the spot in the lovely gardens of the ruined Abbey, where you may meet a monk who'll tell you all about it.

☎ 01284 830385

62 *Wide open spaces in the heart of East Anglia.*
Honeypot, near Eye.

Acres of parkland, lakes and conservation areas; next to the site two hundred acres of common land. Fish here for carp, bream, roach and rudd, walk for miles or maybe bring a kite – this is perfect country for it. The tranquility here is tangible. Venture outside the gates and you'll find the three essentials of British life – pub, tea shop and fish and chip shop. Venture even further and you'll find you're right in the heart of East Anglia – perfect for exploring.

☎ 01379 783312, fax 01379 783293

63 *Landscaped garden site near ferry port.*
Low House, near Ipswich.

Camp in a beautiful garden, packed with ornamental trees and plants, arches and bowers, doves, rabbits, bantams and guinea fowl. Wilder wildlife all around, and sea fishing seven miles away. Close to Constable country, and close too to the port at Felixstowe, this is a lovely spot for a night or an enchanting base for a holiday. Temporary membership of a popular nearby sports/social club available to visitors.

☎ 01473 659437, fax 01473 659880

64 *Parkland of a baron's residence. Haveringland Hall, Cawston, near Norwich.*

In the beautiful grounds of Haveringland Hall, once the home of a baron; one of the homes of the present Queen is nearby, as is that of her ill-fated predecessor Anne Boleyn. An Earl has a seat here and Nelson his birthplace. Nobles and commoners alike have long loved the evocative Norfolk coast, with birds to watch at Blakeney and crabs to eat at Cromer; try boating on the Broads or the fun of the seaside resorts. The site provides seclusion, peace and quiet, with its woodland walks and huge lake for a spot of quiet fishing.

☎ **01603 871302**

65 *Seals, coast and bird reserves. Long Furlong Cottage, near Holt.*

Seals and wild birds abound at Blakeney; this is a site for lovers of wildlife and walking. The proprietor is a Life Fellow of the Royal Society for the Protection of Birds, and is delighted to welcome kindred spirits to this magical corner of Norfolk. Peaceful and orderly, the site sits in beautiful rolling countryside with coastal towns and all the treasures of the East Anglian interior not far away. A lovely tranquil spot for exploring a memorable area.

☎ **01263 740833**

66 *Banks of a beautiful river. The Willows, Scole.*

On the banks of the River Waveney, this is a lovely spot, bordered by willows and a haven for birds, with its own little island. Fish in the river, and if the water's deep enough navigate it by canoe or inflatable. The village of Scole dates from Saxon times; the Romans built a wharf and a substantial town here, and dropped coins in the water to excite future generations. The ancient coaching inn is splendid. A truly charming little corner.

☎ **01379 740271**

67 *Historic towns of East Anglia. Swan's Harbour, near Norwich.*

Explore East Anglia's famous towns and villages from here – Norwich, Cambridge, Walsingham and Wymondham are close, as is King's Lynn on the coast and the Queen's estate at Sandringham. Nestled on the banks of the River Yare, the site is sensitively landscaped and pretty, blending well with the Norfolk fields and big skies. Lots of space; walk for miles and savour it, all through the year.

☎ 01603 759658

68 *Stagecoach stop on the Great North Road. Road End Farm, near Stamford*

Stamford is a hidden treasure of a town, arguably the best place of all to stop on the Great North Road between London and Edinburgh; the town's lovely buildings merit a day's exploration. Not far from here too is Rutland Water, the British Isles' largest man-made lake with 3,000 acres of water and all sorts of water sports. Stay nearby at Road End Farm, at any time of the year – it's pretty in the frost and pretty in summer too.

☎ 01780 63417 Fax: 01780 65656

69 *Across the Humber. Silver Birches, Barton-on-Humber.*

The Viking Way long-distance footpath marks the steps of these ancient and somewhat anti-social explorers, who no doubt would have appreciated the famous suspension bridge that now crosses the Humber Estuary. This comfortable little site sits at the foot of it, and makes an excellent base for exploring either side. Nearby Barton-on-Humber is full of history and exceptional churches, and a lovely Nature Reserve spreads along the banks of the river for miles.

☎ 01652 632509

70 *Antiques, architecture and famous landscapes.*
Willowmere, near Sudbury, Suffolk.

This is Lovejoy country – TV fans of the loveable rogue will recognise settings for his antique-dealing antics everywhere in this beautiful Essex-Suffolk border country. Flemish weavers and wool merchants came here and brought wealth; splendid churches and fine pastel-painted houses abound. Willowmere is a lovely little site surrounded by trees and meadows in the Stour valley, near Sudbury where Gainsborough was born. Nearby Long Melford (unmissable) has two stately homes, a cathedral-sized church, antique shops a-plenty and good eateries/pubs serving local Greene King beer. Walk three miles along disused railway track to Lavenham – just as lovely.

☎ **01787 375559**

71 *Dramatic landscapes and cosy corners.*
St. Margaret's, near Woodbridge, Suffolk.

What wonderful, atmospheric scenes there are around Woodbridge, evocative of Holland with its barges and Old Master skies. This is a coast of creeks and inlets, pretty villages, fresh fish and cosy pubs, a world of its own with a mood of its own. St. Margaret's site is just two miles from a river and three miles from the sea, in beautiful countryside right in the heart of it. Wonderful for fishing and boating; excellent walking and (flat) cycling country, with horse riding and golf nearby. At the house you can buy fresh milk and dairy produce, and 150 yards away in the village the 'Sorrel Horse' serves fine food and fine ales.

☎ **01394 411247**

72 *Sailing, cycling and safaris.*
Chestnut Farm, near Southwold.

Six miles from elegant Southwold and perfect for sailing on the Broads. Camp in a grassy meadow surrounded by trees behind an old farmhouse; this is a friendly little site ideal for exploring this timelessly special part of East Anglia. Dream country for cyclists, with miles of empty country lanes and only the gentlest of slopes. Theoretically good fishing in the River Hundred, except that the plant life's taking over – people come back with more water lilies than fish! Explorers can go on safari at the Suffolk Wildlife Park next door (giraffes, lions and some pretty wild water lilies).

☎ **01502 740227**

73 Forestry Commission camping in Thetford Forest.

Thorpe Woodland, near Thetford on Suffolk/Norfolk border.

Camp in East Anglia with the Forestry Commission, who have a simple, undeveloped site deep in Thetford Forest Park. As well as that special atmosphere that comes from being in the woods, there are lovely walks and lots of scope for cycling. Plenty of wildlife, and plenty of room for junior explorers to mount their expeditions and relish this natural, healthy environment a world away from traffic and exhaust fumes. This is a good base for roaming the Norfolk Broads and for discovering lovely East Anglian towns like Bury St Edmunds.

☎ 01842 810271 or 01842 751042

74 For exploring the atmospheric Fenland country.

Whaplode manor, near Holbeach, Lincolnshire.

The Fens are dramatic, atmospheric and studded with intriguing little towns and villages often overlooked. This is prime agricultural country, famous for its flower festivals, particularly the tulip festival, early in May; good bird-spotting territory too. Whaplode Manor is a fine eighteenth century building offering flat, grassy and sheltered camping for discoverers of this mysterious region (and all the advantages of having a bar on site). Very close is the coast where a King lost his jewels in the Wash.

☎ 01406 422837 Fax 01406 426824

75 Riverside tranquility not far from Skegness.

Riverside, Wainfleet, Lincolnshire.

Peace and quiet on this neat and friendly little site near Skegness and the lovely Lincolnshire Wolds. By the side of the unpolluted river Steeping, which teems with roach, perch, bream, tench, pike and gudgeon, and not far from the wonderful nature reserve at Gibraltar Point, the mouth of the river. At the source of the river is Somersby, where Tennyson was born and which inspired his poem 'The Brook'. Contrast this peace and poetry with car, motorbike or go-kart racing nearby, plus all the fun of the fair at Skegness.

☎ 01754 880205

76 *Little farm site in the Evesham fruit country. Broadclose Farm, near Worcester.*

People come to the Vale of Evesham on fruit-picking holidays – the area's famous for its apples, strawberries, pears and plums. Mrs Steel's quiet little ten-pitch site on Broadclose Farm is a lovely spot for exploring a lovely area. High up, it looks west to the Malvern Hills, the Clee Hills and the hills of Wales. Lots of lovely excursions – try the Royal Worcester porcelain factory at Worcester, or Broadway, so perfect it looks like a film set. And of course, fascinating Stratford-on-Avon.

☎ **01386 792266**

77 *Much ado about Shakespeare. Dodwell Park, Stratford-upon-Avon.*

"I'd give all my fame for a pot of ale", wrote William Shakespeare. One wonders if he ever had any idea just how famous he'd be. The whole world comes to Stratford, where you can see his birthplace, learn about his life and times and see his works performed at the famous theatre. All this and pots of ale too, and good shops and narrowboats to watch as they negotiate the lock in the middle of the town. Dodwell Park is a peaceful and relaxing site, close to it all. Find time for Warwick too; steeped in history, it's one of the most beautiful towns in this heartland of England.

☎ **01789 204957**

78 *Overlooking scenic Dovedale. The Alamo, near Ashbourne, Derbyshire.*

A very pretty site high above the village of Thorpe looking across to Dovedale andThorpe Cloud. Walk on the hill, or hire a bike from the Visitors' Centre at nearby Carsington Water – there's a good bridle path here (two pubs in the village for essential refreshment). Two miles from Ashbourne, a pleasant market town. A blissfully tranquil base for the less-than-tranquil but hugely enjoyable delights of Alton Towers, twenty minutes' drive away.

☎ **01335 345731**

79 *Riverside camping near Northamptonshire village. Mill Marina, Thrapston.*

Six pleasant riverside acres, with open fields all around. Moorings and slipways; watch the boats or bring your own. Fishing too. This is a relaxed and friendly site, full of interest, near the lovely Nene Valley with its walks and cycle routes. Relax here by the riverside or explore Northamptonshire with its stone houses, pretty villages and handsome towns. All sorts of attractions all around, and nearby, the village of Thrapston for all you need. Buy a caravan here, or get hooked on the life afloat and buy a boat!

☎ **01832 732850**

80 *Pub camping in Shropshire's Mini-Switzerland Engine and Tender Inn, near Ludlow.*

People come on holiday from all over to what this site owner describes as 'just a green field'. What you can't see from the picture is that this green field is attached to the 'Engine and Tender' inn, which has all the usual pub camping advantages plus a restaurant. What you can see is that it's in the glorious Clun Valley. This is the area known as 'mini-Switzerland', a paradise for walkers and for hang gliders, and a little pocket of spectacular scenery near the historic border town of Ludlow. Hardly surprising that folks come from far and wide – it's just beautiful.

☎ **01588 660275**

81 *Peace in an orchard on Herefordshire border. Park House, near Ludlow.*

Camp in an orchard on this tiny little site halfway between Ludlow and Leominster just off the A49. There are only six pitches, so you can be sure of tranquility in this prettiest of settings. Good ale and pub food is to be had all around, and there's a 'Little Chef' two miles away for full-blown English breakfasts with no cooking! This is a friendly little place where you're welcome to bring pets in an area of timeless towns and villages – Herefordshire countryside, with its orchards and black and white houses is a real and unspoilt pleasure. Two National Trust properties close by.

☎ **01584 711558**

82 *Spectacular hills of Shropshire.*
Small Batch, near Church Stretton

If you need to ask what makes Shropshire special, you've obviously never been there, say the proprietors of Little Batch! Known as Little Switzerland, you can walk for a month and take a different walk every day. This site's been there since 1928, through three generations – they think it's 'absolutely wonderful', and aren't at all surprised that everybody keeps coming back. Look at the picture. Need we say more?

☎ 01694 723358

83 *Wildlife and wide-open vistas.*
Park Grange, near Bridgnorth

A family home, offering a warm country welcome from Biscuit the pony, a pondful of frogs, goats, chickens, cats and quite a few bees. Honey to buy here, and eggs; catch-and-return fishing, wild flowers and wild birds. Country life at its most fun and most soul-reviving, for all ages, whether you stay for a night or a month. For a contrast, visit nearby Ironbridge, ponder on the Industrial Revolution and what we've done since.

☎ 01746 714285 OPEN ALL YEAR

84 *Pubs, pints and Black Country heritage.*
The Blount Arms, near Kidderminster

Friendly pub with a warm welcome for campers on the edge of the scenic Wyre Forest near Ludlow's famous castle. All the benefits of camping a la beer garden, including bar meals and children's play area. Don't just pass through – if you've time, discover this region with a style and heritage of its own, captured in the Black Country Museum. Worcester has canals, choir festivals and china – the Royal Worcester works is here, open for fasicnating visits and bargain buys. An ideal base.

☎ 01299 270423

85 *At the foot of the Malvern Hills. Kingsgreen, near Great Malvern.*

Lots of footpaths lead up into the lovely Malvern Hills from this excellent little site at the foot of them. A 200-acre working farm, with fishing available on site, it has spectacular views over Herefordshire to the Brecon Beacons and the Black Mountains of Wales, to Shropshire and the escarpment of the Cotswolds. Explorers based here will enjoy the towns, too – Malvern, Ledbury, Tewkesbury all have stories to tell. The Forest of Dean is a dramatically-coloured haven of peace all through the year. Easily reached from the M50, Kingsgreen has superb facilities for disabled people too.

☎ 01531 650272

86 *Scenery, wildlife and heritage. Glencote, near Leek, Staffordshire.*

A pretty site at ancient Cheddleton near Leek, the natural gateway to the beautiful Churnet Valley. Spectacular scenery honeycombed with pleasant walkways along which the waters of the Churnet cascade over miniature waterfalls and where flora teem and fauna abound. Walk the Cauldon Canal towpaths and watch colourful narrowboats, heron and kingfisher. Every sort of outdoor pursuit here (attractive little pond for coarse fishing on the site too) – plus much of North Staffordshire's proud industrial heritage to see. Truly the heart of England.

☎ 01538 360745, fax 01538 361788

87 *Traditional farm camping in Shakespeare country. Mill Farm, near Shipton on Stour, Warwickshire.*

Bring your gypsy caravan, or an ordinary one will do – this friendly farm in rolling-hill countryside provides a lovely little corner for exploring a wonderful area. A mere mile takes you to the Rollright Stones, and sixteen to Stratford-on-Avon, dedicated to the bard and a must on any explorer's itinerary. The Cotswolds too are close. Warwickshire is full of lovely villages and particularly lovely pubs; take time to discover it. Lots of canals too.

☎ 01608 684663

88 *Lots and lots of room with a view.*
Sycamore, near Matlock, Derbyshire.

Four acres of lovely lawns at this quiet and very scenic little site near Matlock in Derbyshire. Lovely views too over distant hills tempting you to go off and explore them. Which you should; there are treasures to be found. Take to the river at Matlock Bath, look at the river from the bridge at Ashworth in the Water and be dazzled by the outlook from Monsal Head. At Chesterfield be amused by the church spire. Explorers of the great indoors will love Chatsworth House and Haddon Hall.

☎ 01629 55760

89 *Camp at famous Grand Prix racing circuit.*
Park Farmhouse, Donington Park.

Camp next to the competitors' entrance at Donington racing circuit and watch life in the fast lane from a leisurely spot in the slow one. See also the fascinating Grand Prix Collection, a celebration of eighty years of Grand Prix racing and the world's largest collection of Grand Prix cars. Next time you're on the M1 try this highly original site and turn a routine stopover into an experience in its own right. Plenty of rural peace and quiet all around, Castle Donington and Derby nearby.

☎ 01332 862409, fax 01332 862364 OPEN ALL YEAR

90 *The great outdoors and plenty of it.*
Haytop Country Park, near Matlock, Derbyshire.

A sixty-five acre park, part of the old Alderwasley Hall Estate, rural and undeveloped with woodlands, meadows, two streams and the River Derwent flowing through. Ten species of mammals are seen here regularly, and sixty types of birds, and fishing can be arranged. Bring a little boat or canoe if you have one and make the most of it. This is a place for losing yourself in the simple pleasures of the great outdoors with all the room you need for stretching legs and unwinding. Some intriguing attractions to visit round about too. OPEN ALL YEAR

☎ 01773 852063

91

Forestry Commission camping in the Forest of Dean.
Woodlands, near Christchurch.

A natural, undeveloped site run by the Forestry Commission in the Forest of Dean. Secluded pitches in ancient oak woodland. Walk from here down through lovely forest to the spectacular valley of the river Wye. A lovely cycle path follows the river into Monmouth, scene of many a border bust-up between the English and the Welsh. This mysterious forest is really worth exploring – traces of its surprisingly recent, surprisingly industrial past are there to unearth.

☎ **01594 833376**
(all Forestry Commission Forest of Dean sites).

92

Estuaries, valleys and bridges.
Hogsdown Farm, near Dursley, Gloucestershire.

The Severn Estuary, with its hills, riverside meadows, wildfowl and useful bridge into Wales, is not far from here; the Wye Valley, Berkeley Vale and the Cotswolds are close too. Historic market towns abound. This little site is a rural retreat for country lovers and a smashing base for touring; it's convenient for the M5 and the A38 and open all year. Open, level countryside (cyclists take note) with distant views. B&B at the farmhouse too.

☎ **01453 810224**

93

Wye valley – river and pasture.
Lower Ruxton Farm, King's Caple, Herefordshire.

Sheep may safely graze in these lush pastures, and canoists (reasonably) safely canoe on the adjoining river. Lower Ruxton Farm invites you to share its rural tranquility and explore the Wye Valley – by canoe, or on foot via the many lovely walks. Close to picturesque Ross-on-Wye and historic Hereford. Herefordshire is delightful territory for explorers – spectacular black-and-white beamed houses and wonderful cider.

☎ **01432 840223**

94 *A Yorkshire oasis. Springs Farm, Lothersdale.*

The Wars of the Roses raged between Yorkshire to the east of here and Lancashire to the west; fortunes were made and industrial heritage founded in the working towns to the south. Difficult to imagine though. Nearby Airedale gave its name to a curly dog, enough excitement for this calmest of Yorkshire havens. This is the gateway to the Dales and the Lakes, not far away to the North. Or simply the route to peace and quiet and calm.

☎ 01535 632533 Fax 01756 799848

95 *North Yorkshire's exhilarating Dales. Shaw Ghyll, near Hawes.*

Vertical-take-off lambs abound in the intoxicating atmosphere of the Yorkshire Dales. Here the air's fresh and there's room to bounce around whether you've two legs or four. Try the Pennine Way (best on two) not far away for spectacular walking, or tour the fells and dales. Yorkshiremen say theirs is God's own country, and, on a glorious day here, who'd argue? Good country for wool, for spinning and for knitwear; cheesy Wensleydale streches out to the east. This site is small, secluded and friendly, bordered by a trout stream.

☎ 01969 667359 Fax 01969 667894

96 *Dukes, vets and film crews. Howgill Lodge, near Skipton.*

Wharfedale, in North Yorkshire, is truly spectacular. Ramble by the river or follow the fells, wander in woodland, tread the nature trails and, whatever else you do, find Simon's Seat and the Valley of Desolation. Film-set fame as the location for Emmerdale Farm and the James Herriot stories is totally understandable when you're here. This is the Duke of Devonshire's Bolton Abbey estate; Ann and Bernard Foster live in the middle of it, and offer wonderful camping plus B&B and self-catering accommodation.

☎ 01756 720655

97 'Last of the Summer Wine' country. Earth's Wood, near Huddersfield.

'Last of the Summer Wine' was filmed round here, so TV fans will know just how beautiful it is. The site is quiet, secluded and thick with bluebells in the season; from it an old coach road leads through the woods to the picturesque village of Cawthorne. A country museum and a wildlife sanctuary are nearby, as is the Yorkshire Sculpture Park. This is a serene and lovely place, on the southern slopes of the Dearne Valley, perfect for exploring the Peak District.

☎ **01484 863211/864266, fax 01484 863820**

98 Off the motorway and into real Yorkshire. Stubbings Farm, near Leeds

Only ten miles from Leeds and you're in the midst of all this. Totally uncommercialised farm site looking over Wharfedale, with woods and paths to explore on foot or by bike. Towns to discover too – Skipton and Holmfirth are not far, and Otley's only a mile and a half with all its trappings of civilisation. If you can drag yourself away.

☎ **01943 464168** 

99 Valley walks and distant views. Usha Gap, near Richmond.

Spot the caravan, deep in this delicious Swaledale valley, beside the beck. This is Usha Gap, between the lovely villages of Muker and Thwaite – glorious walks, and shops and cafes when you get there. Buttertubs Pass takes you to Hawes, seven miles away. Mrs Metcalf's delightful farm site is friendly and well-organised – a perfect base for exploring this loveliest of landscapes. The Pennine Way and Coast to Coast walks pass nearby.

☎ **01748 886214** 

177
174
175
176
172
173
171
170
169
168
167
165
166
162
164
161
163
160
159
101
158
108
157
102
156
123
111
201
155
154
115
106
118
200
119
117
116
100
198
127
104
197
195
121
120
99
109
122
95
128

100 *Would-be dowsers – and everybody else – welcome! West Roods, Barnard Castle.*

A happy, friendly place where you can learn to dowse! You can watch the milking too, on this working farm (lady cows only, no bull, we're assured) or play 'farm style' table tennis, cricket, badminton and practice golf. If you can take your eyes off the view, that is – on a clear day you can see the North Sea fifty miles away, and with binoculars watch the ships waiting to enter Hartlepool. Overlooking Barnard Castle in the foothills of the Pennines.

☎ 01833 690116 (long ring please)

101 *Cosy haven in rugged Northumbria. Proctor Steads, near Alnwick.*

Sheltered, cosy and comfortable, one mile from the sea and the spectacular beaches this coast has to offer. Castles abound, including extraordinary Alnwick with its opulent interior. Just a few miles away is the causeway to magical Holy Island, on which sits Lindisfarne Priory. Near the site a warm and welcoming country inn provides an ideal staging point for explorers returning to base.

☎ 01665 576613

102 *Secluded farm on the Pennine Way. Demesne Farm, Bellingham.*

Bellingham sits on the edge of the river which flows through a magnificent valley from Kielder Water to the Tyne. This working farm is on the famous Pennine Way long-distance path, bordering the Cheviot Hills, in dramatic and unexploited countryside. The Romans did a lot of walking round here too (not for fun) and built Dere Street nearby; they also built Hadrian's Wall, in a (pretty futile) attempt to stop the Brits and the Scots squabbling. Walk around its ruins today, and imagine what it must have been like.

☎ 01434 220258

103 *Busy ports and quiet havens. Mill Farm Country Park. Skipsea.*

Half a mile from the sea, with coastal footpaths and historic ports to visit, including bustling Bridlington, this little site is perfect for lovers of things maritime. Much to do for landlubbers too; shops, markets, museums and leisure centres a-plenty. All this from a peaceful farm site, near the tranquil Wolds; enjoy watching the birds on nearby meres and at the famous R.S.P.B. site at Bempton Cliffs. The farm offers explorers all the information they need to discover it all. Or simply stay on the farm, and enjoy the walks and the welcome.

☎ **01262 468211**

104 *Yorkshire's fascinating coast. Hollins Farm, near Whitby.*

One for explorers under canvas only – on the edge of the moors near the Yorkshire fishing port of Whitby. The town has a spectacular setting and an evocative atmosphere; Dracula thought so (visit the graveyard). The Cleveland Way follows a fascinating coast. Inland the villages are lovely; the local one has, among other things, three pubs. From this simple little farm site you can walk, ride horses and try the steam railway.

☎ **01947 897516**

105 *By boat into York. Riverside, Bishopthorpe.*

Two miles up the River Ouse from York sits this lovely riverside campsite – with its own riverbus service into the heart of the city! Camp in beautiful surroundings and tranquility, fish, launch your boat or hire one; venture out and explore the coast, the moors and the dales. And as for York, enter it afloat – the Vikings did. The waterfront is lovely, and the city has enough to see for a month of holidays. Nearby Ripon is quieter, apart from its town crier; walk along the towpath and watch the boats go by.

☎ **01904 704442/705812, fax 01904 705824**

106 *Durham, county and city.*
Viewley Hill, Bishops Auckland, Co. Durham.

Not for nothing is this called Viewly Hill. Explore the cycle routes and forest drives; walk the rolling hills or the valleys below; this is countryside on a big scale. The stately fortified city of Durham is not far; built on a near-island in the river Wear (not the easiest plot for building anything), it's massive cathedral was built to resemble that of Caen, on the orders of William the Conqueror. Mrs Hodgson's tiny little site is in a perfect spot; expect to hear the curlew and the peewit, and probably an odd owl hooting nearby. Fishing is close at hand (as is the Brown Horse Inn).

☎ **01388 730308**

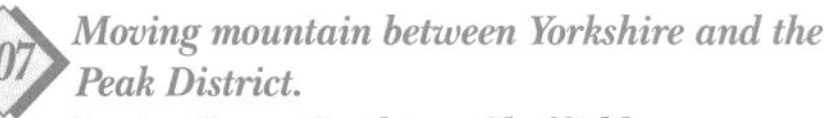

107 *Moving mountain between Yorkshire and the Peak District.*
Rowter Farm, Castleton, Sheffield.

Wonderful guided trips through 'show' caverns near here – see Speedwell Cavern by boat, and at Blue John cavern find the stone of that name used for jewellery. Above ground you're in lovely hill country, where if you climb a little you'll see Edale. Camp on this sheep and cattle farm from where you can walk for miles and miles; Yorkshire's on one side and Buxton, Bakewell and the Peak District are on the other. When you go there, keep an eye on one of the hills – it's called the 'Shivering Mountain' because, it seems, it never stops moving.

☎ **01433 620271**

108 *Forestry Commission camping near Scottish border.*
Kielder, The Borders.

In the heart of Britain's largest forest, three miles from the border with Scotland, you'll find one of the Forestry Commission's lovely natural sites. Several forest trails and cycling routes start from the Visitor Centre at Kielder Castle; you can sail, go fishing or take a ferry on Kielder Water of follow a Forest Drive over remote and beautiful moorlands. A beautiful place to camp, surrounded with history – hill camps, Roman forts and castles abound. The great outdoors at its most exhilarating and interesting.

☎ **01434 250291 (season),**
01434 220242 (other times)

109 *By the side of the River Swale. Low Whita, Richmond, Yorkshire.*

Farm site in a glorious riverside spot deep in a valley. Excellent pot-holing country – enthusiasts will enjoy a plunge into the famous 'Butter Tubs'. Much for less subterranean souls to enjoy too, including walking, cycling, pony trekking and fishing. Plenty of craft shops in this part of the world, including lovely woollens from Swaledale; nearby Hawes boasts a ropemaker. And Tan Hill has the highest pub in England – definitely worth dragging yourself out of a pothole (or anything else) for.

☎ **01748 884430**

110 *Stately homes and security squirrels. Nostell Priory, near Wakefield, Yorkshire.*

In the grounds of splendid Nostell Priory, a National Trust house open to the public with spectacular architecture and a superb collection of Chippendale furniture. Take a walk around the famous rose gardens or amble along the lakeside walk; the shrubs and trees are lovely. This cheery and welcoming place teems with woodland creatures; the manager asks for your help in respecting the rules and looking after them, and warns you that she's fitted the squirrels with security cameras! A beautiful place, and a lot of fun, very well placed for exploring the ridings of Yorkshire.

☎ **01924 863938**

111 *Handful of pitches on Northumbrian farm. Ashcroft Farm, near Hexham.*

Only five pitches on a sheep and beef farm not far from majestic Hexham, a historic abbey town with Roman remains to visit and much else. Camp in the valley next to the South Tyne river; cross by the footbridge for lovely bankside walks, one of which takes you to fine National Trust house Allen Banks. A chance to see traditional Northumbrian farm life and to explore this wild and dramatically beautiful county. The squirrels round here are red ones.

☎ **01434 344409**

112 The Peak District at its loveliest. Cottage Farm, near Buxton.

Right in the heart of the glorious Peak National Park. Hilly, rocky country yet relatively gentle; no need to be a super-fit, super-keen walker to enjoy this. Feast your senses here; rivers tumble over waterfalls, and some of England's finest stately homes beckon. Tour by car if you prefer; Buxton and Bakewell are not far away, with plenty to see and do. Or simply stay put and relish the beauty of it all. Mrs Gregory's farm campsite, not far from the A6, bids you welcome.

☎ **01298 85330**

113 Stately homes and gardens – spectacular Peak District. The 'Grouse and Claret', near Bakewell.

TWO stately homes (Chatsworth and Haddon Hall) within walking distance, for lovers of fine houses and glorious gardens. The Peak District National Park, for lovers of the great outdoors. This is the home of the Bakewell Tart (a pudding, not a person) and of the mysterious business of dressing wells. Explore it all from the riverside grounds of the warm and welcoming 'Grouse and Claret', whose extensive facilities and menus are at your disposal, including full English breakfast, the ultimate indulgence for the more hedonistic explorer. Comfy camping, cosy bars, B&B and facilities for families.

☎ **01629 733233** OPEN ALL YEAR

114 Canals and calm – just off the M6. Laundsfield, near Lancaster.

Canals wander in a world of their own, through time-warp countryside sometimes within minutes of big cities. This tiny, lovely site in the midst of fields is only half a mile from the M6 (junction 33) and one-and-a-half miles from Lancaster University, and yet is totally quiet and calm. Walk for miles – this is the Trough of Boland, the scenic route between Yorkshire and Lancashire, with its hills, rivers ands treams. Or follow the canal to Glasson Dock, a major canal boating centre; watch the hustle and bustle of boats coming and going, and maybe try one for yourself.

☎ **01524 751313** OPEN ALL YEAR

115 *Debate and drama in the Border Country.. Camelot, near Carlisle, Cumbria.*

This is the Debateable Land – the bit fought over between England and Scotland in the Border Wars. The multi-million-pound Tullie House Museum in nearby Carlisle is an unforgettable experience taking you back in time to those stormy days. Turbulent runaway lovers fled to Gretna Green, just over the border, where they could be married. Debate rages over new research that suggests that Longtown is the burial place of King Arthur. Perfect peace from all this drama, plus a perfect place for investigating it all, at this welcoming little site, set in beautiful countryside off the scenic route to Edinburgh.

☎ **01228 791248**

116 *Real farm camping in ancient Westmorland. Hawkrigg Farm, near Appleby, Cumbria.*

A working farm with wonderful views, this tiny site is close to Appleby, originally the county town of the ancient county of Westmorland. Much to see in the town, surely one of the most picturesque in northern England. With the Northern Pennines as backdrop and the river Eden running through, this is lovely country indeed, and its sheltered position gives it a mild and dry climate. In June permanently travelling folk converge here for the centuries-old Horse Fair. As well as lots of lovely walks, short and long, there is the Cumbria Cycle Way, a treat for two-wheeled travellers.

☎ **01768 351046**

117 *Lovely lakes in lovely Lakeland Burns Farm, near Keswick.*

Not for nothing is this district named after its lakes. Their beauty is in their mirror-clear water reflecting the dramatic scenery all around them, nowhere seen so clearly as in this view, taken two miles from Burns Farm. Camp here near Keswick in the quieter part of Lakeland – the views from this little farm site are described as 'the nicest you could possibly have'. Right on a cycle route, there's a river for fishing and just down the road a famous stone circle to explore.

☎ **017687 79225**

118 *Heart of Lakeland farmhouse. Gill Head, near Penrith.*

This family-run hill farm has a lovely sheltered campsite with stunning views. B&B and self-catering accommodation too (ideal for mix-and-match holidays) in this particularly pretty 17th century farmhouse. Easy to reach; leave the M6 at junction 40 and plunge into the heart of Lakeland on the road to Keswick. Walking, golfing, fishing, pony trekking, sailing and everything else this deservedly-famous region has to offer.

☎ **01768 779652**

119 *In the steps of poets. Violet Bank, near Cockermouth.*

Walk in Wordsworth's footsteps here. He was born in nearby Cockermouth – visit the house and this lively little market town too, just up the road from this meadowland site with magnificent views. It's pretty and bursting with all the shops, cafes and restaurants you'll need. This less-developed northern part of the Lake District is walking country par excellence. Hosts of golden daffodils in spring only, but views and sights to intoxicate the senses all year round.

☎ **01900 822169**

120 *On the shores of the lake. Pier Cottage, Coniston.*

Never any room here, alas, in school holidays – the picture shows you why! On the banks of Coniston Water, one of the most famous of the Lakes, with its pier and beaches this really is something special. Beg, borrow, steal or inflate a little boat and make the very most of it. Coniston village is a short and scenic walk away. Phone to find out when there's space, and reorganise the year around it!

☎ **015394 41497**

121 *Trains, Tarzan and timeless peace. Fisherground Farm, Eskdale, Cumbria*

Arrive here by miniature railway, if you like! Its own halt on the 15" Ravenglass and Eskdale Railway, connecting with the normal-sized network, gives this site a truly 'outpost' feeling. With a magical adventure playground for kids (of the pond, tree house and Tarzan rope variety), set in the heart of the magical adventure playground for adults that is the Lake District. More attractions than you can count all around – yet here, simply tranquility and spectacular scenery, fresh air, walks, camp fires and calm. This is Lakeland at its most peaceful and most beautiful – still more sheep than people.

☎ 01946 723319

122 *Hills, dales and lovely villages. High Laning Farm, Dent, Cumbria.*

On one side the Lake District and on the other the Yorkshire Dales; double paradise for real explorers. Fell-walking par excellence and a thousand other things to do, outdoors and in; down the road the picture-book village of Dent, rich in history, with pubs, cafes, shops and local crafts. Jim and Margaret offer you the warmest of welcomes to their working farm (fresh produce to buy). If you don't know this soul-reviving part of the world, sample the essence of it here. Bring your boots, forget your cares. Holiday cottage to let too.

☎ 015396 25239

123 *Sixty acres of countryside and conservation. Oakbank Lakes Country Park, near Carlisle.*

Spot the campers! They're somewhere deep in this sixty acres of wide open space with its twenty-five acres of lakes; a paradise for fishermen, expert or beginner. Trout, carp, tench, bream, there to be caught or to outwit you – tackle and tuition are available. Conservation is the watchword here; spot the birds, too. There's a bird sanctuary, observation hides and a game bird breeding unit. Roam the grassland walks and deciduous woodland, far from the madding crowds. Or venture off to nearby Hadrian's Wall or Gretna Green.

☎ 01228 791108 (phone/fax)

124 *Perfect haven for motorway travellers*
Strawberry Wood, near Macclesfield, Cheshire.

Woodland camping, with fishing on the site and lovely walks from it, not far from the M6. An ideal stop if you're heading south of Birmingham or north of Manchester – deep in these woods the cities and motorways seem a world away. Worlds even further away are scanned from the giant telescopes of Jodrell Bank, which you can see from the site. Chester, built by the Romans, is close by, a lovely town well worth a visit, and the Cheshire countryside is full of scenic surprises. A friendly, welcoming site in a perfect spot for travelling North.

☎ **01477 571407**

125 *Lovely Lancashire valley – just off the motorway.*
Gathurst Hall Farm, near Wigan.

Walk the towpaths, eat and drink at the Navigation Inn and go horseriding, all within five hundred yards of this little site in the wooded River Douglas valley. This is the edge of the Lancashire Plain, picturesque, full of little country pubs, tranquil – and just off the M6! Whatever else you do here, visit Wigan Pier, which graphically and fascinatingly demonstrates, with working exhibits, life as it was lived in industrial Lancashire in days gone by. This is an excellent 'overnight' site – but you'll miss a lot if you don't stay longer!

☎ **01257 253464**

126 *In the grounds of Northwood Hall.*
Northwood Hall, near Chester.

Northwood Hall was built in the 1880s for a blind vicar – today you can camp in its eight acres of glorious grounds. There are particularly beautiful mature tress here, oaks, spruce, sycamore and ancient, spectacular horse chestnuts. Nearby is the Delamere Forest. This is walking country – try the famous Sandstone Trail, and canal country too. Walkers serious or otherwise will be glad to know that there are plenty of pubs within strolling distance of the site; Chester is seven miles away, and is pretty and interesting enough for a day's exploration at least.

☎ **01829 752569**

127 *Lakeland valley camping. Bayesbrown Farm, near Ambleside.*

Be dwarfed by the landscape here. Real out-of-doors camping right on the Cumbria Way at the start of the Great Langdale Valley; whichever way you go from here the scenery's stunning. This is a place for stretching your legs, filling your lungs with fresh air and rejoicing in the great outdoors – with several friendly pubs nearby for enjoying the great indoors. A working farm (sheep and cattle); the farmhouse offers comfy B&B too.

☎ 015394 37300

128 *Quite simply, real camping. Birchbank, near Ulverston.*

Only five pitches on a sheep farm. Bordered by a stream, this is one of those simple, tranquil corners we dream of finding. Good walking country and good for cycling too, with lots of bridleways and manageable slopes. Lovely expeditions from here to some of Lakeland's most interesting attractions; try the Owl Centre, Beatrix Potter's house or perhaps the sculptures in Grizedale Forest.

☎ 01229 885277

129 *Seaside fun from tranquil base. Melbreak, near Morecambe Bay.*

Over by the coast, three miles from Morecambe Bay, where all the fun of the Great British Seaside Resort is yours to enjoy – it may exhaust you, but it certainly won't bore you! And you can do it all from this small, neat and quiet site, cunningly placed to be far from the madding crowds, handy for the bright lights and only one mile from the fine sandy beach at Middleton. Real explorers will enjoy discovering this area's attractive little villages too.

☎ 01524 852430

130

Welsh mining valley reborn.
Afan Argoed, Afan Forest Park, near Port Talbot.

The last coal mine closed in this beautiful South Wales valley in 1970; now thousands of acres of glorious forest park cover it. An information centre, gift shop and mining museum tell you about the past, the story of the park's development and the wealth of things to enjoy today. From the tiny campsite by a disused railway line you can walk 30 miles of marked forest trails and cycle 25 miles of bike paths, fish for trout, go orienterring and spot an amazing variety of birds. The drumming of woodpeckers has replaced industry's clamour. Truly beautiful.

☎ 01639 850564

131

Heads of the Valleys.
Clydach Gorge, near Gilwern.

Between Abergavenny and Ebbw Vale, just of the Heads of the Valleys road – this is the language of the great South Wales mining heritage. The language too of an area stunningly scenic. This little site at Clydach Gorge is on the edge of the Brecon Beacons National Park. Seek out the lovely little Monmouthshire and Brecon Canal, which winds its shallow way through secret places, as is the way of canals. An area for wandering and discovering, with wonderful walks and the mountain-ringed market town of Abergavenny nearby.

☎ 01633 832733 (after April 1997: 01633 644844)
Fax 01633 644800

132

A farm welcome in the hillsides.
Grawen Farm, near Merthy Tydfil, mid-Glamorgan.

Picturesque mountain, forest and reservoir walks inside the Brecon Beacons National Park. A wealth of history in the town of Merthyr Tydfil and the valleys. Mrs Pugh offers you a warm welcome to her site on Grawen Farm. The Welsh have a famous song in which they promise to 'keep a welcome in the hillsides'. Don't leave this country without hearing the famous male voice choirs, born of the mining tradition and with some of the most moving music in the world. Look around you and you'll see what inspired them.

☎ 01685 723740

133 *Up in the peaks of the Brecon Beacons. Pencelli Castle, Brecon.*

Take a boat trip on the Monmouthshire and Brecon Canal from the marina near this friendly, family-run site – the canal runs close to it. Walk the tranquil towpath, or, if you're feeling upwardly mobile, walk the hills – the highest points of the Brecon Beacons are very close. Natural beauty whichever way you go – a paradise for nature lovers. Fresh farm produce close by. Facilities for the disabled on this site.

☎ **01874 665451**

134 *Cosy country pub in remote hill country. 'Cross Inn'/Black Mountain, near Llangadog.*

An area steeped in folklore, history and tradition, deep in the Brecon Beacons National Park looking toward the Black Mountain. Magnificent walking country with lakes, reservoir, rivers, caves and waterfalls all around. Wonderful wildlife, including the rare Red Kite. Make your base camp this little site belonging to the 'Cross Inn', a friendly pub with all facilities, including excellent meals, where they'll help you to enjoy it all to the full.

☎ **01550 740621** OPEN ALL YEAR

135 *Cheery Welsh farm welcome. Coedhirion Farm, near Carmarthen.*

An overnight stop which often ends up lasting much longer! Pull off the main route into South Wales and discover a real treasure. A Welsh farm, which you are welcome to explore (wellies not needed!), with camping in a woodland setting – no nightlife, says Mrs Evans, but plenty of wildlife! Plenty of lovely walks. Wonderful breakfasts available at the farmhouse, which also offers B&B, and two friendly seventeenth-century inns in the village. Welsh spoken here, as well as English – CROESO CYNNES I COEDHIRION!

☎ **01267 275666**

136 *Ferries and family trees in spectacular Pembrokeshire.*

Mount Pleasant, near Narberth.

Stop here for the Fishguard-Rosslare ferry to Ireland – it's just off the B4313, the quietest (and best) route. Don't leave Wales though until you've discovered the county of Pembrokeshire. Its coastline is spectacular and its castle-studded countryside is fascinating. This little 'off the beaten track' site is perfect for enjoying the views and the walks, and maybe a spot of fishing. And while you're here, learn a little about genealogy and find out how to go about tracing your family tree.

OPEN ALL YEAR

☎ **01437 563447**

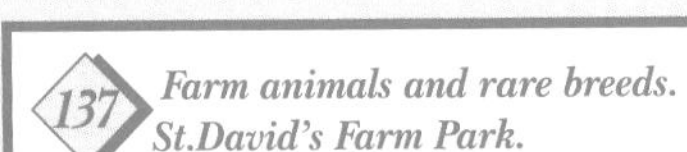

137 *Farm animals and rare breeds.*

St.David's Farm Park.

Come and enjoy life on a farm with a difference – this is the largest and most varied collection of rare breeds in Wales. Four-horned sheep, shaggy cattle and stripey Iron Age piglets, shire horses to ride and bunnies to cuddle – everything here is 'hands-on', and children (of all ages) love it. Special events, demonstrations, restaurant and gift shop – and you can camp here too. This very special site is only half a mile from beautiful Whitesands beach too!

☎ **01437 721601**

138 *Conservation area on the Dyfed peninsular.*

Dolbryn, Newcastle Emlyn.

A very pretty little site near Newcastle Emlyn in Carmarthenshire, perfect for exploring the Dyfed peninsular. A quiet rural setting in an idyllic valley (conservation area) with much to discover; wander up to the nearby vineyard, or venture further out to the coast of this scenic peninsular. Cardigan, the birthplace (one assumes) of the button up woolly, is not far; pleaure craft and fishing boats moor at the quays. There's a wildlife lake on the site, and room to let off steam with tennis, badminton etc too – the friendly owners have equipment you can borrow at the house.

☎ **01239 710683**

139

On coastal path by Newport Bay.
Tycanol Farm, Newport, Pembrokeshire.

Another one of those pictures that makes the words superfluous. Not far from the town of Newport, this little site's right on the coastal path next to the beach at Newport Bay on the Pembrokeshire coast. Real explorers could walk for miles on the Pembrokeshire Coast Path, or swim for miles, or go beachcombing, or simply sit and gaze out across the sea to Ireland. Or go off to hunt for the 5,500 year old Coetan Arthur burial chamber (not where you'd expect it). They could stay just for one night and then catch the ferry from Fishguard. Seem an awful shame, though, wouldn't it?

☎ **01239 820264**

140

Mid-Wales, timeless and beautiful.
Fforest Fields, near Buith Wells, Powys.

Follow in the steps of the Princes of Wales, and see the castles they fought over; more humbly, tread the paths of the drovers and discover the little market towns they visited. This is timeless country, mid-Wales, with its majestic hills and deep wooded valleys. High in the hills are the spectacular Elan Valley dams, where red kites and buzzards compete for thermal currents – everywhere there are sheep. George and Kate's happy little site, spacious and peaceful, nestles in a bowl in the hills far from the noise of traffic or the lights of towns. A mile takes you to the village; there's a village store and Post Office, and a most welcoming pub that serves the best food for miles.

☎ **01982 570406**

141

Farm between Lampeter and coast.
Tan-Yr-Alt Farm, near Lampeter.

Simple farm camping between the interesting little town of Lampeter and a fascinating part of the coast. Dylan Thomas lived at New Quay; you can catch mackerel there, or take a boat trip out to sea to watch dolphins and porpoises play. Injured and oil-soaked sea birds are rescued at the Bird Hospital, which you can visit. Further along at Aberaeron is a Honey Bee Exhibition! Much to see and do, and lovely walks; Mr and Mrs Davies have B&B at the farmhouse too.

☎ **01570 470211**

Real
Exploring in WALES

142 *Heavenly scenery and a devil's bridge.* *Pantmawr, near Aberystwyth.*

Spectacular views from this little site – it overlooks the Rheidol valley, the sea and the mountains! Walk and ride to your heart's content, or go fishing just down the road; There's a narrow gauge railway too (you can see that from the site too!) for trips through this lovely scenery. Or go into Aberystwyth, a pretty little coastal town with all mod. cons. and yet still plenty of original character. Three miles down the road is a bridge built by the Devil – or rather, three bridges, one on top of the other, spanning a gorge across a great river. Thereby, no doubt, hangs a tale (forked, presumably).

☎ **01970 880449**

143 *A friendly welcome in peaceful mid-Wales.* *Cringoed, Llanbrynmair, Powys.*

Slate mines, castles, railways, craft centres, nature reserves and a Centre for Alternative Technology are down the road from here. These donkeys aren't interested in ANY sort of technology – but they are interested in meeting the folk who come to stay at Cringoed. Five acres of simple rural camping alongside the river Twymyn, with beautiful views of the soft mid-Wales countryside. Good for walking, birdwatching, pony trekking, fishing, lakes and coast.

☎ **01650 521237**

144 *Superb setting in southern Snowdonia.* *Doleinion, near Tywyn, Gwynedd.*

Be bowled over by camping in this countryside, which gets on all the calendars. In southern Snowdonia, and an area of Special Scientific Interest, this delightfully pretty little site is surrounded by wild cherry blossom, bluebells and rhododendrons, with riotous colours in autumn and a special magic in winter. It has its own trout stream, and is at the start of the 'Minffordd Path' rising to mighty Cader Idris. Go fly-fishing for brown trout in the lake close by, explore the coast, find the narrow gauge or the slate caverns or simply enjoy the wildlife and the setting. Lots of information on site, and a lovely welcome.

☎ **01654 761312** OPEN ALL YEAR

145 *Working farm in cormorant country.*
Gesail Farm, near Tywyn, Gwynedd.

A true working Welsh farm, with a camping field in front of the lovely eighteenth-century farmhouse B&B too). The scenery is breathtaking, although as ever the sheep and cattle munching contentedly don't seem to notice it. This is the foot of 'Bird Rock' in Snowdonia, cormorants come inland to nest here, returning to the sea for food. Walkers, cyclists and rock-climbers will love it here. Explorers in search of the unusual might find peat beds, a dragon stone, Arthur's labyrinth and a gold mine, among much else.

☎ **01654 782286**

146 *At the foot of Cader Idris.*
Tynbryn, near Tywyn, Gwynedd.

There's a monument near here to Mary Jones, who in 1794, aged ten years, walked barefoot on mountain paths all the way to Bala where she'd heard she could get a copy of the Bible, then virtually unobtainable. Another Mary Jones lives here now, and welcomes you to her little camp site, in a lovely field with a river flowing along the side, from where you can see one of the oldest castles in Wales. Fish in a mountain lake, walk, cycle and ride in this valley at the foot of Cader Idris; it's wonderful.

☎ **01654 782277**

147 *Lovely riverside base for wonderful excursions.*
Bryn Gwyn Farm, near Bala.

Walk along a riverside footpath into Llanuwchllyn village where there's a village shop and a hotel well-known for its excellent and reasonably-priced food; from the station, catch the Bala Lake narrow gauge railway and journey along the length of the largest lake in Wales, stopping perhaps for a picnic at Llangower. Try Bala Town's intriguing Town Trail, or perhaps go canoeing or rafting at the National White Water Centre. So much to do from this excellent little riverside site with glorious mountain views and free fishing, centrally positioned for exploring Snowdonia and the coast.

☎ **01678 540687**

148 *On the road to Betws y Coed.*
Glan Ceirw, near Corwen, Clwyd.

A super spot for exploring north Wales, on the A5 twelve miles from Betws y Coed. This is a friendly, family-run site, with nine pitches in a lovely rural setting – the river Ceirw runs through the park. Good territory for fishing and sailing, on the edge of Snowdonia not far from the North Wales coast. The village is a mile away, and pretty Ceirw House, which also offers B&B, has a bar where everyone is welcome for drinks. A convenient and comfortable touring base.

☎ 01490 420346

149 *Bear's birthplace deep in Snowdonia.*
Cae Du, Beddgelert, Gwynedd.

An escape from the world, deep in the heart of Snowdonia, with access to the high peaks from the site. Spectacularly scenic, undeveloped and unspoilt, by the side of the river Aberglas in this paradise for walkers, climbers, fishermen, explorers and lovers of the outdoors. Half a mile from a much-photographed village village, where lived the creator of Rupert the Bear. Would be one of North Wales' best-kept secrets, were it not for the other fans of such magical places that already know about it, so you'll need to book in advance. Well worth the planning ahead.

☎ 01766 890345 OPEN ALL YEAR

150 *Between the sea and the mountains.*
Llwyn Bugeilydd, Criccieth, Gwynedd.

Clean beaches, a thirteenth century castle, a rabbit farm and no traffic lights. This is Llwyn Bugeilydd, where you can camp in farmland sheltered by mountains. It's free from stress, with unspoilt natural beauty, tiny quaint villages and warm, welcoming people. Haul yourself off the beach and try the seaside towns of Criccieth and Pwllheli, or maybe listen to some jazz in Porthmadog. And if you're too relaxed to do anything else, venture into the amazing and unlikely village of Portmeirion. A lovely farm site for enjoying all this and avoiding the madding crowds.

☎ 01766 522235

151 Quiet farm camping near splendid Caernarfon.
Tyn Rhos, Caernarfon, Gwynedd.

Caernarfon – the river fort. 'Fort' hardly does justice to spectacular Caernarfon Castle, scene of the investiture of the Prince of Wales in 1969. 'River' barely describes, the Menai Strait either. This Lleyn Peninsular is a wild one, crossed by an ancient pilgrim path and scattered with prehistoric remains and old churches. Wonderful exploring country, inland and along the coast. Tyn Rhos Farm has twenty pitches and panoramic views, an excellent little haven and base camp, with the beach only two and a half miles away.

☎ **01286 830362**

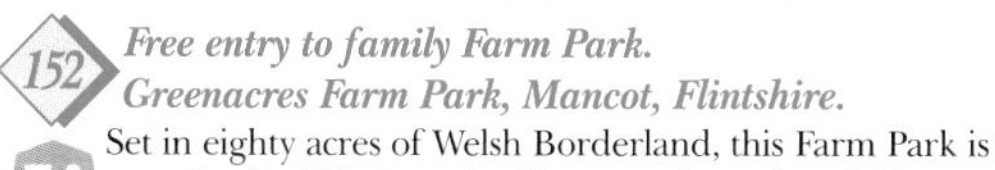

152 Free entry to family Farm Park.
Greenacres Farm Park, Mancot, Flintshire.

Set in eighty acres of Welsh Borderland, this Farm Park is paradise for kids. Puppies, kittens, guinea pigs, chicks, goats, deer, llamas – a long list of animals, rides, playgrounds, shows, shop, cafe and very much more. Stay on the campsite here and access to the Farm Park is completely free! Perfect for a treat for youngsters on a touring holiday, or as a special expedition. Much to see all around, too – near the River Dee and Flint Mountain, with Wales on one side and historic Chester on the other.

☎ **01244 531147 (phone, fax)**

153 Across the bridge to atmospheric Anglesey.
Garnedd, Brynteg, Isle of Anglesey.

Sunset over the Isle of Anglesey, 'Mother of Wales'. Here the dawn with the sun rising over Snowdonia is beautiful, the sunsets are beautiful, the harvest moons are breathtaking. This is a time-warp place, not modernised, not spoilt, where things move slowly and people have time to talk and to listen. David and Mary love doing just that with their visitors – in fact, they love everything about their island off the northernmost tip of Wales. Go and camp by their traditional Welsh farmhouse and find out why. And while you're there, see if you can find the Bog Bean.

☎ **01248 853240**

154 *Looking out to sea on the Solway coast. Castle Point, by Dalbeattie, Galloway.*

Camp facing out to sea, and when the tide's out walk across the bay to the bird sanctuary on Rough Island. Panoramic views across to the Lake District and the Isle of Man from this little site on a headland where an ancient fort once stood. Walkers exploring the cliffs and the surrounding farm will find some of the best scenery on the Solway Coast, plus three beaches within a mile. Energetic explorers will find pony trekking, mountain biking, forest walking, hill walking and fishing close by. Plus tennis and golf – problem here is keeping your eye on the ball and not the scenery.

☎ 01556 630248 (April to October), 01241 860433(out of season).

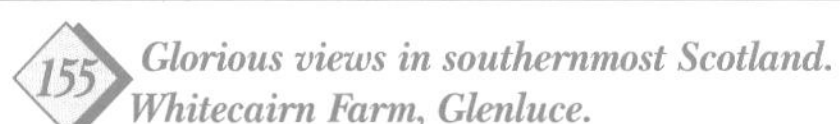

155 *Glorious views in southernmost Scotland. Whitecairn Farm, Glenluce.*

Here, you can hear the silence. Peace, quiet and spectacular views, five minutes from the sea. Lovely colours and lovely gardens, thanks to the warming effect of the Gulf Stream – good golf courses too, of the 'turn up and play' variety. This site's on a farm, with ten touring pitches, and is only ten minutes from the ferry to Ireland, which you can visit on a day trip. A taste of days gone by in this part of the world – the High Street in Stranraer has no big stores, and in Wigtownshire traffic lights (apparently) don't count.

☎ 01581 300267 (phone and fax)

156 *Scenic farm and wildlife centre. Barnsoul Farm, near Dumfries.*

Roam over 250 acres of woods, heath and field on this scenic farm and wildlife centre, famous for its bird population – over 120 species recorded. Half an hour's walk takes you past Old Water to tumbling Routin Brig, through bluebell woods and up to the historic Communion Stones. Walk or cycle to Glenkiln Reservoir, and discover statues by Henry Moore and Rodin sitting serenely in their unique rural setting. A lovely place to stay, with all you need nearby and easy access by boat, plane, train and road.

☎ 01387 730249 (phone and fax)

157 *Rob Roy and Braveheart country. Mains Farm, near Stirling.*

Seek out this farm site at the edge of Thornhill village with panoramic views over the Carse of Stirling to the Fintry Hills. Follow the Trossachs Trail through a scenic area of lochs, glens and mountains made famous by the story and film of Rob Roy. Explore Royal Stirling with its historic castle and step back in time with a climb up the Wallace Monument, where you'll learn the story which inspired the epic film 'Braveheart'. A real find.

☎ **01786 850605**

158 *By the river Doon in Burns country. Skeldon, near Ayr.*

A lovely little twenty-pitch site about seven miles from Ayr, birthplace of Scotland's most famous poet, Robert Burns. 'Auld Ayr wham ne'er a town surpasses for honest men and bonie lasses' was his description. A trip to this major and very handsome resort to find out just how bonie the lasses are is a must; the coastline too round here is pretty special, and extinct volvano Ailsa Craig can be seen from the shore and visited by boat. Lots of gardens with sub-tropical plants in this region too, thanks to the Gulf Stream. Camp by the side of the river Doon - and enjoy the trout fishing on site!

☎ **01292 560502**

159 *Doctor Livingstone, one presumes. Newhouse, near Lanark.*

A friendly farm site with its own fly-fishing trout loch, no mean attraction. Explorers able to drag themselves away from this will find themselves in the 'garden valley' of the river Clyde, where among very many other things (and beautiful scenery) they will find the birthplace of David Livingstone. Visit Scotland's noisiest museum, go down a lead mine and, whatever else you do, discover New Lanark, an award-winning reconstruction of an eighteenth-century mill village where you'll be shown around by a ghost.

☎ **01555 870228**

160 *Lovely welcome in fascinating Fife.*
Woodland Gardens, near Leven.

Regulars from all over the world keep coming back here, it's so friendly and helpful – one of them even married into the owners' family! It's peaceful, comfortable and and safe whether you're two or a hundred and two, and this is what the scenery looks like (there's a volcano in the background). Coastal, hill and forest walks, fishing villages, castles, palaces, mansions houses and gardens to visit, and golf courses everywhere – it's only twelve miles to St. Andrews. Stop for a night, or make it a base for a whole Scottish holiday (Edinburgh and Dundee aren't far). You'll be welcome either way.

☎ 01333 360319

161 *Essence of Scotland*
Balquhidder Braes, Lochearnhead, Perthshire.

Red deer frequently graze in and around the park here, roe deer and foxes can be spotted, buzzard and grouse are common and orchids grow prolifically. Wonderful hill walking starts on the doorstep, mountaineering and trout fishing are close by. The private water supply comes from a bore-hold in the ground and tastes like nectar. A dream site for lovers of country pursuits, peace and quiet (no facilities, though, for children). This is the place to try wearing the kilt – the owner does.

☎ 01567 830293 Fax 01567 830363

162 *Deep in the glorious Angus Glens.*
Nether Craig, near Blairgowrie, Perthshire.

Seek out this site deep in the secret world of the Angus Glens. Silent, remote places at first glance, they're home to warm, friendly, characterful communities. Tour by car or bike, and find plenty of surprises – castles, ruins, Pictish relics. Fishermen can choose loch or river, and there's always another hill to climb or view to admire in this unspoilt countryside with panoramas of the Strathmore Valley. Nether Craig's a super little site, set in farmland, with its own woodland walk and riding, trekking and golf on the doorstep.

☎ 01575 560204 Fax 01575 560315

163 *Scotland's beautiful West Coast.*
Arduaine, by Kimelford, Argyll.

Sea frontage here, with a small beach and safe swimming – moorings and launching for small boats too. Across the clear waters of the bay (enjoyed by seals, otters and oyster catchers) are the islands of Shuna, Scarba and Jura. This lovely coast, warmed by the Gulf Stream, is home also to palm trees and rare plants – and only 400 yards from the site are the world-famous Arduaine Gardens. You could follow the Argyll Scenic Route from Loch Lomond to Fort William, take a wildlife cruise to uninhabited islands and whirlpools or cross to Ireland on the ferry. Or feast on seafood at the local hotel. Or just sit and gaze at it all.

☎ 01852 200331 Fax 01852 200337

164 *Spectacular setting near coastal Oban.*
Oban Divers, Oban, Argyll.

This glorious site's an extension to a family diving business in coastal Oban, nearby. Superb setting, as you'll have deduced from the picture, with a stream running through (definitely NOT deep enough for diving!) and lots of places for kids to play. Golden eagles were seen last year, and a ten-minute walk takes you to a fresh water loch where you can catch brown trout. Campers washed or blown out can dive into under-cover log cabins and cooking facilities – or one of the many pubs in Oban. Friendly, cheery, interesting and not to be missed.

☎ 01631 562755 (phone, fax)

165 *Looking west to the islands.*
Fiunary, Morvern, Argyll.

Amidst magnificent Highland scenery, looking across to the Isle of Mull , this small and friendly site has its own safe beach for swimming and launching small craft. Wander for miles through idyllic countryside and spot rare wildlife, or at low tide reach some of the offshore islands of foot, or take one of the forest walks that start form the site. From nearby Lochaline village you can get a ferry to the Isle of Mull; this is the ideal base for exploring the islands of Iona and Staff too, plus Ardnamurchan, the most westerly part of the British mainland. A magical spot.

☎ 01967 421225

166 *Cheery relaxed camping in historic Glencoe.*
Red Squirrel, Glencoe, Argyll.

Lots of laughter, lots of friendship – the owners describe themselves as 'eccentric' and their farmsite in world-famous Glencoe as totally different, refreshing and very homely! The squirrels and the international clientele love it – camp fires on the river bed, river swimming, canoeing, salmon fishing, a sea loch pier just over a mile away. All the scenery and drama of Glencoe; seventeen miles to Ben Nevis. Bring your sense of humour and enjoy the happy chaos and camping as it used to be!

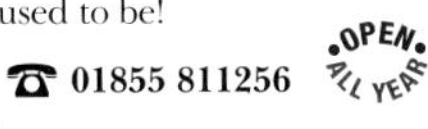

☎ **01855 811256** OPEN ALL YEAR

167 *A Hebridean paradise.*
Newdale, Tobermory, Isle of Mull

This is Tobermory, on the Isle of Mull, an enchanted place which'll work its Celtic magic on you. The simple, very friendly little Newdale campsite is just a mile and a half from this scene. Roam the island, with its scenery and wildlife; wonderful crafts and Celtic to buy. Try a 'ceilidh' – it means 'a friendly gathering', and can't be described! Find Fingal's Cave and see what inspired Mendelssohn; go sea angling, or cruise the islands and see puffins, guillemots, razor bills, otters, seals, dolphins, porpoises (and if you're lucky whales and basking sharks). A glorious place to camp.

☎ **01688 302306 (phone and fax)**

168 *Walled garden on island nature reserve.*
Garden House, Isle of Coll, Inner Hebrides.

Camp in the walled garden of this isolated farm in the middle of an RSPB nature reserve. This is the Isle of Coll in the Inner Hebrides – from the hill above, you can see the outer ones. This is an island with history – Mrs Graham will tell you what happened to the hazel trees in 1858 ('Coll' is Gaelic for 'hazel') and about the 'Mullachs', marauders from Mull. A beautiful and atmospheric place, home to corncrakes, buzzards, merlins, peregrines, windchats, wheatears and redshanks, and sometimes visited by sea eagles. Fishing, tennis, camp fires and barbecues.

☎ **01879 230374** OPEN ALL YEAR

169 *Looking over the sea to Skye.*
Portnadoran, Arisaig, Inverness-shire.

A lovely little site beside this house, overlooking the islands of Skye, Rhum, Eigg and Muck – there are daily boat trips to all of them. Skye is the one you can see here – follow in the wake of the royal fugitive who fled there 'over the sea' and touch a little Scottish history. This is a wonderful place for boating and fishing, and a paradise for children, with miles of coat to explore; inland there are lovely hills to walk. Nearby Arisaig village has shops, meals and pub.

☎ 01687 450267 (phone and fax)

170 *Near Aviemore in the Cairngorms.*
Dalraddy, by Aviemore, Inverness-shire.

On a traditional Highland sporting estate near the famous ski centre of Aviemore, in the Cairngorms. Wonderful loch and river fishing, clay pigeon, riding and much more to do, or simply enjoy walks round the estate and take in the spectacular scenery and views. The Spey valley is lovely; as well as its obvious winter attractions it has a great deal of history. Find a Druid stone circle, a flying bell, a fifteenth-century island castle and some wonderful museums. A good site in an interesting place.

☎ 01479 810330 Fax 01540 651380

171 *Farm camping on the shores of Loch Ness.*
Borlum Farm, Drumnadrochit, Inverness-shire.

This is where the Loch Ness monster lives! Borlum Farm is close to the shores of Loch Ness in Drumnadrochit, home of the Loch Ness Monster Exhibition Centre. Camp behind the farm (25 pitches and lovely views of Glen Urquhart) and spend your day trying to spot the famous beastie. Or help with the homelier beasties on the farm – there are lambs to care for, ponies and sheep to be rounded up and eggs laid by unruly hens to be searched for. The village is pretty, the welcome is warm and the Great Glen scenery is stupendous. And who knows – you MAY see the monster!

☎ 01456 450220 Fax 01456 450358

172 *Valley beauty spot in the Highlands. Spindrift, near Nairn.*

Stop and explore the Highlands from this lovely little family-run site hidden in the Nairn valley, surrounded by deer, badgers and otters, yellowhammers, kingfishers and ducks. Close to the site of the Battle of Culloden, with four inhabited castles open to the public within fifteen minutes' drive; impregnable Fort George on the Moray Firth coast makes a dramatic outing too. Walk along the river from the site, through beautiful and historic scenery, right into the centre of the resort of Nairn, with its sandy beaches. Go fishing, or take a boat trip and search for dolphins.

☎ **01667 453992**

173 *Forestry Commission camping in the West Highlands. Balmacara, Kyle of Lochalsh.*

An ideal touring base for Skye and the north-west Highlands, this site is within easy reach of picturesque Eilean Donan Catle and Gavin Maxwell's 'Ring of Bright Water'. The soaring new bridge to Skye is only a few minutes away. Sheltered, secluded and near the sea, it's set in parkland and open wood and is a haven for wildlife. Peace, quiet, a variety of forest walks and some of the most magical views in the world. Another lovely Forestry Commission site.

☎ **01599 566321**

174 *Little site at John O'Groats. Stroma View, John O'Groats, Caithness.*

"Go to John O'Groats and turn left" say the instructions for finding this site. Camp at this most famous of extremities; there are fifteen pitches, a place for kids to pay and a little shop which sells among other things Caithness glass and Arran pottery. The site overlooks the island of Stroma and you can see the Orkneys from here. Dramatic, wildly beautiful – you haven't 'done' Britain till you've been here!

☎ **01955 611313**

175 *Harbours, hauntings and mermaids.*
Oldshoremore, by Lairg, Sutherland.

Fifteen pitches on a working croft, on the coast fifteen miles south of Cape Wrath. Clean, golden beaches, safe for bathing, and beautiful hill and loch scenery. This is a conservation area where wild plants grow along the cliffs and thousands of birds nest on offshore islands. Two miles away is a busy harbour with its fleet of fishing boats. Sandwood Bay, a little to the north, is reputedly haunted, and the last mermaids were supposed to have been seen there. Remote, beautiful and fascinating.

☎ **01971 521281**

176 *Another world.*
Eilean Fraoich, Shawbost, Isle of Lewis.

Iain MacAulay, who owns this little site, is a crofter and a genuine Harris Tweed weaver who can weave yards a day. Visitors are welcome in the weaving shed when he's finished work, and he'll show you how it's done. He and his family wash clothes and cook meals for visitors too, even delivering them to tent or caravan, and give whatever help and information they can, unstintingly. This is the way of things on Lewis, where people count for more than belongings or appearances. Discover more than a fascinating island here – this is a philosophy and a way of life apart.

☎ **01851 710504**

177 *The Orkney Islands, wild and wonderful.*
Point of Ness, Stromness, Orkney.

Orkney has treasures which set it apart from the rest of the world. These seventy islands have villages, burial chambers and standing stones that pre-date the Pyramids; extraordinary landscapes, wondrous wildlife, sea-pounded cliffs, rich green pasturelands and vivid carpets of flowers. Unique, dramatic Stromness has houses built into its granite hill and others built on stone piers protruding into the harbour. The food tastes so fresh you realise what your palate's been missing. Twenty pitches here on the Point of Ness, a wild little corner of paradise.

☎ **01856 873535, fax 01856 876327**

178 *On lovely headland near Waterford.*
Boatstrand, Annestown, Co. Waterford.

Situated on glorious Dunabrattin Head, with magnificent views of the rugged Waterford coastline. This is an unspoilt place, with sheltered sandy coves and beaches and wildlife in abundance; explorers can seek out a ruined castle, an ancient dolmen, Celtic burial grounds and tombs. The harbour offers every imaginable kind of messing about in boats; Cathy's homemade cakes and pies can be bought nearby. The site is small and relaxed, and has its own craft shop.

☎ **051 396 110**

179 *Deep in an ancient forest.*
Glensheland Forest, Cappoquin, Co. Waterford.

Brand new site (opens April 1997) in beautiful Glensheland Forest in the Blackwater Valley. Follow the riverside past bridges and waterfalls walk up to an abbey where the monks of an enclosed Cistercian order, clad in traditional sandals, pursue their time-honoured way of life. Follow their example and opt for a quiet time in the serenity of this lovely place, where wildlife proliferates, free and protected. Or join in a host of forest activities from orienteering to heritage trails. A lovely woodland haven.

☎ **058 60419 Fax 058 60435**

180 *Ferries and the Viking coast.*
Jasmine Villa, Carrigtwohill, Co. Cork.

A friendly, neat little site not very far from the Cork/Swansea/Roscoff ferry terminal, convenient yet very secluded and very quiet. Beaches and fishing within three miles, plus a golf course, a wildlife park and a heritage centre. This is a fascinating coast, which fascinated the Vikings so much they kept coming back (and not necessarily improving the amenities). Linger a while and discover it all; this nineteen-pitch site is an excellent base.

☎ **021 883234**

181 *Kissing the famous Stone.*
Stone View, Blarney.

If you don't know the legend of the stone at Blarney, go there and they'll tell you all about it – at length. This lovely little site (the only one in the area) overlooks the stone and its castle, in what must be one of Ireland's most visitable villages. Seekers after traditional souvenirs and knitwear will be in heaven when they discover the huge mill building packed to the roof with them next door; there are good restaurants and pubs with traditional music every night. Only ten minutes from Cork, too.

☎ 021 385167

182 *By the Healy Pass in South Kerry.*
Creveen Lodge, Lauragh, Co. Kerry.

Two miles from the sea and a mile from the Old Sibin pub (and plenty of others not far either), in the beautiful scenery of South Kerry. Walk or cycle from this little rural site to rivers, lakes and mountains – the coast road is stunning. Dereen Gardens to visit, or just make the most of the countryside – the view from the Healy Pass on the Kerry-Cork border is second to none. A lovely place to stop on the way west (if you can bear to move on).

☎ 064 83131

183 *Beach site on the Ring of Kerry road.*
Wave Crest, Caherdaniel, Co. Kerry.

The seashore in front of this campsite, a beachcomber's paradise, leads to the beach at Rath. Lots of small harbours and beaches around here; the clear, warm waters are perfect for diving. Archeological sites abound; there are ancient copper mines, a prehistoric ring fort and an abbey on an island for fascinating expeditions. Not to mention singing pubs. This is the famous Ring of Kerry, a road which circles the Kerry peninsular through wonderful scenery linking picture-book villages and harbours. Walk it, cycle it or drive it – don't, whatever you do, miss it.

☎ 066 75188 (phone and fax)

184 *Friendly farm park with home-cooked food.*
Nore Valley, Bennettsbridge, Co. Kilkenny.

A working farm which is open to visitors – here you'll be encouraged to help with the animals, hold them and take a ride on a tractor. It's a lovely place, overlooking the scenic river Nore – you can follow it for a two mile riverside walk on the farm. Explorers with healthy appetites take note – there's fresh, home-baked produce available daily here, and if you come in June, July or August you can start the day with a cooked Irish breakfast. Good area for history lovers – lots to see – and there are plenty of craft centres too.

☎ **056 27229 (phone and fax)**

185 *On the way to Tipperary.*
The Apple, Cahir, Co. Tipperary.

Not 'the big apple', just 'The Apple' – a smashing little farm site with orchards to roam and apple juice to buy. Plums, redcurrants, raspberries and strawberries in season too – have a wander round and see for yourself how it's all grown. Tipperary's not a long way from here, nor's Limerick, and the whole area around is packed with delights. Try Cahir with its castle, or Cashel, with its rock and its cathedral; watch gaelic football or hurling and epexerience traditional Irish music and dance. Two tours – one of a crystal factory, one of a distillery. Best to do them in that order!

☎ **052 41459 Fax 052 42774**

186 *Beachside site near Tralee and Dingle.*
Green Acres, Castlegregory, Co. Kerry.

Camp right next to this spectacular beach with its miles of clean golden sands. Excellent windsurfing here for the seriously energetic, and interesting fishing – sea, shore line and deep sea on trawlers! Or just wander along the sands or the lovely hills behind. Good golfing country. This site's on the coast road to Tralee, home of the 'Rose' and famous for its glorious festival of music, dance and drama; it's also near the beautiful Dingle peninsular.

☎ **066 39158**

187 *At the mouth of the Shannon. Aylevarroo, Kilrush, Co. Clare.*

On the Shannon estuary – marina country! A nice little site with all the interest of the coast nearby, yet where you can wake every morning to the sounds of the birds. Excellent swimming and fishing from here, and all along this coast underwater exploration – friendly skin-diving club at Kilkee where they're happy to help visitors. Or simply watch the boats. Where there's boats there's pubs, and Irish ones are famous for their impromptu music and yarn-spinning. Near here is the mysterious Burren, a wild area of geological peculiarities, strange plants, caves and megalithic tombs.

☎ **065 51102**

188 *Tranquil rural setting near Dublin and Rosslare. Moat Farm, Donard, Co. Wicklow.*

A smart little site, on a farm, easy to get to from Dun Laoghaire and within easy reach of Dublin and Rosslare. A clean and comfy place to stop, with all you need nearby, and a campers' kitchen and barbecue areas to make life easy (and fun!). Stride off into the hills, go climbing in the mountains or trying pony trekking or golf. Excellent touring country too, with scenic drives and a number of sites of archeological interest in the vicinity. Friendly and welcoming.

☎ **045 404727 (phone and fax)** OPEN ALL YEAR

189 *Camping on the shores of a picturesque lough. Lakeside, Mountshannon, Co. Clare.*

By the side of spectacular Lough Derg. A wonderful spot, with this glorious lake, mountains, woodlands and islands to enjoy. The charming little village of Mountshannon next door wins prizes for its tidiness, and, to quote the site owner, "has watched the world change and has taken only the best values to add to her charm". A place to enjoy all that's special about Ireland. Explorers with a passion for water will be in their element here – enormous range of water (and other) sports to enjoy. Lovely bike rides and walks too.

☎ **061 927225 Fax 061 927336**

190 *On the banks of the famous Shannon.*
Shannon Cottage

Here you can camp on the banks of the Shannon, just along from O'Brien's Bridge, and take a walk along the riverside through the Bird Sanctuary which adjoins the site. Or go fishing – bait and boats available. Should bad weather force you in from the great outdoors, there's a campers' kitchen on site, and some excellent pubs with inimitable Irish evening entertainment. Lots to do round and about; try Killaloe Heritage Town, just a few miles away. Or get the train to Dublin from the local station, which has day-return tickets at attractive prices.

☎ 061 377118 Fax 061 377966 OPEN ALL YEAR

191 *A place that calls you back.*
Lough Ree East, near Athlone, Co. Westmeath.

This young gentleman's grandfather first came here thirty years ag,o and has been back just about every year since. His father's been coming for fifteen or twenty years; as for himself, he's already a regular. Suggest you go and try this lovely little family-run site, and see why. You'll find it on the shore of Lough Ree, two miles from Athlone, with a trout river bordering it. It has a jetty and a slipway, and boats for hire – excellent for canoeing here, and every kind of water sport. Cruises on the Shannon, pub and shop next door, and all around you the sort of scenery that makes you want to get out and walk in it.

☎ 0902 78561/74414 Fax 0902 74414

192 *Angling, golf and waterside tranquility.*
Hodson Bay, near Athlone, Co. Roscommon.

The exact centre of Ireland! A secluded, wooded site on a farm of one hundred acres on the shores of Lough Ree. The unspoilt lakeshore is a paradise for coarse anglers (especially those with designs on bream) and there are regular trips on the lough by cruiser and hovercraft. On the islands are the ruins of many monastic settlements. Nearby Athlone has a 12th century castle (and all mod cons), and from here there's much to see whichever way you go. Championship golf course bordering the site.

☎ 0902 92448

193 *Real Ireland, warm and open-hearted.*
Hydeoute, Cong, Co. Mayo.

A blissfully peaceful little site in a wonderfully friendly and unspoilt part of Ireland, where the phone numbers have two or three digits and the Tourist Office gives you the name of a local 'contact' who'll be 'only too pleased to help you' discover the area and make contact with the locals. Camp on an isthmus separating two loughs; free (and world-renowned) fishing everywhere, salmon, trout and coarse. Caves, underground rivers (don't miss the 'Rising of the Waters' in Cong village) and archeological sites abound; there's a salmon hatchery to visit too. An area where true Irish culture, with its attendant wealth of song, story, humour and hospitality, is everywhere.

☎ **092 46086**

194 *Site at the beautiful edge of the world.*
Renvyle Beach, Connemara, Co. Galway.

Songs are written about settings like this. Camp by the edge of the ocean at Connemara and watch the sun go down over County Galway. Comb the beach or simply sit on it. There's a breath-taking mountain walk with amazing views of the islands and the mouth of Killary Harbour, and wonderful cycle routes too; there are island tours, handicrafts and sports of all descriptions. Including, of course, that best of all Irish sports, sitting in traditional pubs with traditional music and a glass or two of Ireland's most famous beverage. A glorious site.

☎ **095 43632/43462**

195 *Picturesque town and lovely coastline.*
Tara, Portaferry, Co. Down.

In an Area of Outstanding Natural Beauty overlooking the Irish Sea, with its own path leading down to the sandy beach and rocky coastline. A lovely site on a working farm, where contemplative Charolais cows graze all around. Superb walking on the Ulster Way Path, and along the beach, with a backdrop of emerald fields and the Mountains of Mourne. The cheery little town of Portaferry, two and a half miles away, is picturesque and full of character, and from there you can see Scotland and the Isle of Man. A lovely place to discover.

☎ **01247 728459**

196 *Tiny family site at the gateway to Fermanagh.*
Round Lake, Fivemiletow.

Pitches for twelve caravans and six tents at this super little family site, set in the lovely Clogher Valley, with its green and gentle countryside. There's a backdrop of trees and a small round lake, picnic tables and barbecue area. Near Fivemiletown, this the gateway to Fermanagh, an area with an immensely long history – explore ancient sites such as the Knockmany Cairn, and feel yourself drawn back to the dawn of time. Try the Carleton Trail walking and cycling route, or perhaps the Ulster Way, or visit the ancestral homestead of President US Grant. Lots of local crafts.

☎ 01868 767259 Fax 01868 767911

197 *By salmon river and Atlantic breakers.*
Atlantic'n Riverside, Easkey, Co. Sligo.

Difficult to imagine from the picture, but this peaceful river is about to flow into the sea by a beach which has the best surfing waves in Ireland! This is a place of contrasts; the site, in gentle countryside with the Ox mountains behind, is supremely tranquil; you could while away the day here, with maybe a stroll into the sleepy village or a walk over the fields. Or you could sample the famous trout fishing – and the beaches and the famous waves! Bright lights to be found in the nearby city of Sligo; serenity and interest to be found here from spring onwards.

☎ 096 49001

198 *A welcome from harbourmaster Paddy.*
Kinnego Marina, Oxford Island, Lurgan.

This is Paddy Prunty, Harbourmaster at Kinnego Marina on spectacular Lough Neagh. As well as looking after the welfare of mariners of every kind on this the largest expanse of fresh water in the British Isles, he's also host to visitors at the lovely little camp site by the side of it. A fascinating and convenient place to stop (it's just off the M1 trunk road) whether you're interested in boats, birds, wildlife, history, heritage, scenery or just a beautiful place to spend the night. Explorers trying to choose between dozens of interesting excursions could try the Irish Linen Centre in nearby Lisburn, where you can see how this finest of fabrics is made.

☎ 01762 327573 Fax 01762 347438 Mobile 0374 811248

199 *History and heritage in spectacular setting. Gortin Glen, Omagh, Co. Tyrone.*

In the idyllic rural setting of Gortin Glen, this is a fascinating place to camp. Forests, lakes and mountains are all around, the views are panoramic and the roads quiet (ideal for bikes). Relish the air and the scenery – or discover the history of this intriguing region. There's the Ulster History Park, bringing 10,000 years of it to life, and the Ulster American Folk Park, depicting the links between the Old World and the New. At the Sperrin Heritage Centre, a ghostlike figure will tell you the story of poteen, the legendary Irish drink (which was possibly what reduced the figure to a ghost). A place for learning, or simply enjoying the spectacular setting.

☎ 016626 48108 (phone, fax)

200 *In the walled grounds of a famous manor house. Springhill (National Trust), Moneymore*

Camp in the lovely walled gardens of a National Trust property. This is Springhill, a beautiful seventeenth century manor house, open to the public (and with ground floor wheelchair access); there's a costume museum here too. Woodland walks to explore, and pretty gardens. The camping is basic – and once people have found this very special place, they come back year after year. Wander outside the walls and find nearby Lough Neagh, famous for its marina and its fishing.

☎ 016487 48210

201 *A real Irish welcome. Dungloe, Co. Donegal.*

Céad Míle Fáilte is a phrase you'll see and hear all over Ireland, and that's what you're wished here in glorious Donegal. This is beautiful, wild, rugged region of mountains, lakes and sea; the atmosphere is of peace and tranquility a world away from town life. Try the Croghy Scenic Drive, or take yourself off to explore Aranmore Island. Camp at this nice little site, do a spot of fishing or walking, go down to look at the sea and maybe end the day sharing the company and spontaneous music of the locals in the pub. Site owners Charles and Anne will do everything they can to help you to enjoy it to the full. That's Donegal, and that's Ireland.

☎ 075 21021

Reference Section South East

In this section you will find the essential information you need for contacting and finding sites, together with a listing of the site's facilities, charges, periods of opening and nearby amenities. Prices quoted are normally for a caravan or motor caravan pitch for two persons for one night excluding any supplementary charges for electric hook-ups, awnings, additional persons, etc. For further information please contact the site directly. All sites these days provide the basic facilities of drinking water and a disposal point for chemical waste. Most also have toilets and washing facilities/showers (abbreviated here as 'shwrs'), but some very rural sites deliberately provide only the basics.

1. The Elms, Lippitts Hill, High Beech, Essex. Mr B. Colley. Tel 0181 508 3749/1000 fax 0181 508 9414. 40 ptchs. £8. Mar-Oct. M25 J6. Follow signs to Waltham Abbey, turn L at traffic lights (A112) for 1.3m, 3rd L by Plough pub, 0.5m to site. On site/nearby: toilets, shwrs, payphone, hook-ups, shop, pub, restrnt, free bus to ugrnd stn.

2. Tent City – Hackney, Millfields Road, Hackney, London, E5 0AR. Tel 0181 985 7656; fax 0181 749 9074. 200 ptchs. £5 per person per night. June-Sept.
On site/nearby: toilets, shwrs, laund fac, payphone, cooking fac, shop, pub, rstrnt.

3. Park Farm, Bodiam, East Sussex. Richard Bailey. Tel/fax 01580 830514. 40 ptchs. £5-£6. Apr-Oct. 3m S of Hawkurst on B2244, 3m N of Sedlescombe. Signposted. On site/nearby: toilets, shwrs, payphone.

4. The Merry Harriers, Hambledon, nr Godalming, Surrey, GU8 4DR. Sue & Colin Beasley. 01428 682883. 20 ptchs. £2.50-£10. All year. 1m off A283. Follow signs to Hambledon between Witley & Chiddingfold.
On site/nearby: toilets, shwrs, payphone, meals, shop, pub.

5. The Old Mill, Chalvington Road, Golden Cross, Hailsham, East Sussex, BN27 3SS. D.W. Bourne. 01825 872532. 26 ptchs. £5.50. Apr-Oct. From London turn R off A22 just past Golden Cross Inn. 100 yds on R on Chalvington road.
On site/nearby: toilets, shwrs, hook-ups, payphone, shop, pub, rstrnt.

6. Harwoods Farm, West End, Henfield, Sussex, BN5 9RF. Peter Spear. 01273 492820. 30 ptchs. £3.50. Open: please phone. In Henfield, turn opp White Hart pub in High Street into Church Street. Continue for approx 1.5m till road bends sharply L, in 100 yds straight on into a farm lane. Straight on for 0.5m over cross lane. Site is signed on R.
On site/nearby: drinking water and earth closets.

7. The Cock Horse Inn, Main Street, Peasmarsh, nr. Rye, East Sussex, TN31 6YD. Richard & Eileen Joyce. 01797 230281. 5 ptchs. £10-£12. Mar-Oct. On A 268, 3.5m from Rye. On site/nearby: toilets, shwrs, hook-ups, payphone, shop, pub, rstrnt.

8. Manor Court Farm, Ashurst, Tunbridge Wells, Kent, TN3 9TB. Imogen Berwick. 01892 740279. About 8 persons + 4 caravans with own fac. Max £3.50 per person. All year. 5m east of Tunbridge Wells on East Grinstead road (A264), 0.5m east of Ashurst village, look for farm name. On site/nearby: toilets, shwrs, hook-ups, payphone, breakfast, pub.

9. Brakes Coppice, Forewood Lane, Crowhurst, Nr. Battle, East Sussex, TN33 9AB. Paul & Janet Dudley. Tel/fax 01424 830322. 30 ptchs. From £5.50. Open: phone for details. From Battle take A2100 to Hastings. After about 2m turn R to Crowhurst (Telham Lane) following signs to site up private lane and track.
On site/nearby: toilets, shwrs, hook-ups, laund fac, payphone, shop, pubs.

10. Heaven Farm, Furners Green, Uckfield, East Sussex, TN22 3RG. John Butler. Tel 01825 790226; fax 01825 790881. 25 ptchs. £6 for family (2+2) All year. A275 between Danehill and Bluebell Railway.
On site/nearby: toilets, shwrs, hook-ups, payphone, shop, rstrnt.

11. Whydown Farm, Crazy Lane, Seddlescombe, Nr. Battle, East Sussex, TN33 0QT. Ron Morgan. 01424 870147. 26 ptchs. Mar-Oct. From A21 turn off 100 yds from junction with A229 (opp garden centre).
On site/nearby: toilets, shwrs, hook-ups, laund fac, payphone.

12. Peel House Farm, Hailsham Road, Polegate, East Sussex. Mr & Mrs G.C. Webb. 01323 845629. 20 ptchs. £5.50. Eastr-end Oct. Turn R from A295 to Hailsham. After 10.5m at Bricklayers Arms turn R onto B2104. Site on R 0.5m after Cuckoo Trail. On site/nearby: hook-ups, shop, pub, rstrnt.

13. Horam Manor, Horam, Nr. Heathfield, East Sussex, TN21 0YD. Joan & Mike Harmer. 01435 813662. 90 ptchs. £11. Mar-Oct. On A267, S of Horam village, 3m south of Heathfield.
On site/nearby: toilets, shwrs, hook-ups, laund fac, payphone, meals.

14. Limeburner Arms, Newbridge, Billingshurst, West Sussex, RH14 9JA. Mr. Sawyer. 01403 782311. 42 ptchs. £6.50. Apr-Oct. On A272 Midhurst road, 1.5m west of Billingshurst. Turn L onto B2133. Site is between A272 & A29.
On site/nearby: toilets, shwrs, hook-ups, pub, meals.

15. St. Ives, Butcher Field Lane, Hartfield, East Sussex, TN7 4JX. David Chapman. 01892 770213. 25 ptchs. £6-£8. Apr-Oct. On A264, approx half way between Tunbridge Wells and East Grinstead turn onto B2026 to Hartfield. Site is midway between A264 and Hartfield, on R. On site/nearby: toilets, shwrs, shops, pubs, livery stable.

16. The Red Lion, Old London Road, Dunkirk, Canterbury, Kent, ME13 9LL. Mr & Mrs Lewis-Brown. 01227 750661 (day); 01227 751904 (evening). 24 ptchs. £7-£10. All year. Leave M2 at Junctn 7, take A2 (Dover). Immediately past rndbt, fork L to Boughton. Site on L in 3m in Dunkirk.
On site/nearby: toilets, ch shwr block, hook-ups, pub meals.

17. Pine Meadow, Spratling Court, Manston, Ramsgate, Kent, CT1 25AN. David Steed. 01843 587770. 40 ptchs. £8. Eastr-Sept. Turn N off A 253 Canterbury to Ramsgate road onto A256 twds Margate. In 0.5m turn L onto B2050 twds Manston. In 200 yds turn R into Greensole Lane. On site/nearby: toilets, shwrs, hook-ups, payphone.

18. "To The Woods", Stanwell House, Botsom Lane, West Kingsdown, Nr. Sevenoaks, Kent, TN15 6BN. Mr & Mrs Thomson. Tel/fax 01322 863751. 20 ptchs. From 4.50. All year. 4m N west of Wrotham (A20) turn west into Botsam Lane.
On site/nearby: toilets, shwrs, hook-ups, laund fac, payphone, shop, pub, pool, snack bar.

19. Grange Farm, Military Road, Brighstone Bay, Isle of Wight, PO30 4DA. James Dungey. 01983 740296. 60 ptchs. Mar-Sept. On A3055 between Freshwater Bay and Ventnor. At Brighstone turn L at church into New Road. Site at end of this road.
On site/nearby: toilets, shwrs, hook-ups, laund fac, payphone.

20. Comfort Farm, Pallance Road, Northwood, Cowes, Isle of Wight, PO31 8LS. Mr AE Annott. 01983 293888. 50 ptchs. £6.30. May-Oct.1.5m S of Cowes. From Cowes take A3020, turn R into Three Gates Road at Plessey Radar Test Site. Turn L into Place Road. After 0.25m bear R into Pallance Road. Site is on R after Travellers Joy pub.
On site/nearby: toilets, shwrs, hook-ups, laund fac, payphone, shop, pub, rstrnt.

21. The Spinney, Arlebury Park, Alresford, Hampshire. Mrs. MGM Hide. 01962 732829. 15 ptchs. £5. Mar-Oct.
From Winchester (M3, A34) take A31 twds Alton. Turn L at rndbt onto B3047 to Alresford. Site on L in 0.75m, 2nd entrance.
On site/nearby: shwrs, hook-ups, payphone, meals, shop, pub, rstrnt.

22. Brocklands Farm, West Meon, Petersfield, Hampshire, GU32 1JN. ER Carpenter. 01730 829446. 15 ptchs. £4. All year.
From Petersfield take A272 twds Winchester. In 7-8m at traffic lights turn L onto A32 twds Fareham. Site on L 1.75m.
On site/nearby: shop, pub. Own san essntl.

23. Longbeech, Fritham, Nr. Lyndhurst, Hampshire, SO43 7HH. Forestry Commission. 01703 283771; 01703 282207 for pitch availability in summer. 180 ptchs. £6.50-£8.20. end Mar-Sept. Take B3079 off A31 at Cadnam, then take B3078 via Brook & Fritham.
On site/nearby: own san essntl.

24. Denny Wood, Beaulieu Road, Lyndhurst, Hampshire, SO43 7FZ. 01703 283771; 01703 282207 for pitch availability in summer. 170 ptchs. £6.50-£8.20. End Mar-Sept. On B3056 from Lyndhurst, site 2.5m on R.
On site/nearby: own san essntl, payphone.

25. Huntick Farm, Lytchett Matravers, Poole, Dorset, BH16 6BB. Mr & Mrs. Scrimgeour. 01202 622222. 30 ptchs. £4.50-£6. Apr-Sept. Off A350 Blandford to Poole road. Take turning for Lytchett Matravers and at Rose & Crown pub turn down Huntick Road. Site on R about 0.75m.
On site/nearby: toilets, shwrs, hook-ups, payphone, pub, rstrnt.

26. Haycrafts, Haycrafts Lane, Harmans Cross, Swanage, Dorset, BH19 3EB. Bill & Norma Nelson. 01929 480572. 50 ptchs. £7-£10.50. Apr-Sept. 2m beyond Corfe Castle on A351 at Harmans Cross turn R into Haycrafts Lane. Pass Village Hall on R and site is a further 400 yds on L.
On site/nearby: toilets, shwrs, hook-ups, payphone, shop, pub, rstrnt.

27. Haddons Farm, Haddons Drive, Three Legged Cross, Wimborne, Dorset, BH21 6QV. Mrs KE Jeanes. 01202 822582. 15 ptchs. £4-£5. Apr-Oct. S of Ringwood on A31 at 1st rounbdabout take unclassified road to Three Legged Cross (3.5m), where turn L twds Ferndown. In 0.5m at bus stop turn R down Haddons Drive.
On site/nearby: toilets, shwrs, hook-ups, shop, pub.

28. Highclere Farm, Newbarn Lane, Seer Green, Nr. Beaconsfield, Buckinghamshire, HP9 2QZ. Milson John Penfold. 01494 874505, fax 01494 875238. 60 ptchs. £8.50-£9.50. All year except Feb. M40 Jnctn 2, Beaconsfield. R A355 twds Amersham. 1m turn R to Seer Green, then follow signs.
On site/nearby: toilets, shwrs, hook-ups, laund fac, payphone, shop, pub, rstrnt.

29. Oakley Farm, Penwood Road, Wash Water, Newbury, Berkshire, RG20 0LP. W. Hall. 01635 36581. 30 ptchs. £6. Mar-Oct. From S of Newbury take A343 for 2m. 400 yds after small water bridge turn L before garage into Penwood Road. Site 400 yds on L.
On site/nearby: toilets, shwrs, hook-ups, laund fac, payphone, shop.

30. Mollington Park, The Yews, Mollington, Banbury, Oxfordshire, OX17 1AZ. 01295 750731. 24 ptchs. £5. Mar-Nov. M40 jnctn 11. A423 to Sam. 4m from Banbury on L.
On site/nearby: toilets, shwrs, hook-ups, pub.

31. Bridge House, Clifton Hampden, Nr Abingdon, Oxfordshire, OX14 3EA. Elizabeth Gower. 01865 407725. Apr-Oct. Phone for directions.
On site/nearby: toilets, shwrs, hook-ups, laund fac, pub.

32. Diamond Farm, Bletchington, Oxford, OX5 3DR. Mr Paul Bagnall. Tel 01869 350909; fax 01869 350918. 37 ptchs. £7-£9. All year. Site lies along B4027 road, 1m from A34, 3.5m from jnctn 9 of M40.
On site/nearby: toilets, shwrs, hook-ups, laund fac, payphone, meals, shop, pub, pool.

33. Benson Pleasurecraft, Benson, OX10 6SJ. Robert Allen. Tel/fax 01491 838304. 22 ptchs. £4-£9. Apr-Oct.
Off A4074 Oxford to Reading road, opp B4009 to Benson.
On site/nearby: toilets, shwrs, hook-ups, laund fac, payphone, shop, pub, rstrnt.

34. The White Horse Inn, Priors Dean, Petersfield, Hampshire, GU32 1DA. Roger Datchler. 01420 588387. 100 ptchs. £3. All year. Off B3006 Petersfield to Alton road. On site/nearby: toilets, payphone, pub meals.

35. Wellington Country Park, Riseley, Reading, Berkshire, RG7 1SP. Mrs Morris. Tel 01189 326444; fax 01189 326445. 58 ptchs. £7-£12. Mar-Oct. Between Reading & Basingstoke, signed from A33. 4m S of jnctn 1, M4 & 5m N of jnctn 5, M3. On site/nearby: toilets, shwrs, hook-ups, laund fac, payphone, cafe, shop.

36. Hillcrest, Southampton Road, Whiteparish, Nr. Salisbury, Wiltshire, SP5 2QW. David Tullis. 01794 884471. 2 acres. £6.50. All year. Situated off A36 Salisbury to Southampton road, S East of Whiteparish.
On site/nearby: toilets, shwrs, hook-ups, laund fac, payphone, barbeque area, shop, pub.

37. Stonehenge Touring Park, Orchestron, Salisbury, Wiltshire, SP3 4SH. Derek & Maureen Harnett. Tel 01980 620304; fax 01980 621121. 30 ptchs. £7-£9. All year. Off A360, midway between Salisbury & Devizes. On site/nearby: toilets, shwrs, hook-ups, laund fac, payphone, meals, shop, pub.

38. Alderbury, Southampton Road, Whaddon, Salisbury, Wiltshire, SP5 3HB. Mrs Harrison. 01722 710125. 40 ptchs. £6.50. From Salisbury take A36 Southampton road. On edge of City turn R for Alderbury (1.5m). Park is on L just past Post Office and jnctn. On site/nearby: toilets, shwrs, hook-ups, laund fac, payphone, shop, pub meals.

39. Lower Foxhangers Farm, Rowde, Devizes, Wiltshire, SN10 1SS. Colin & Cynthia Fletcher. Tel 01380 828795; fax 01380 828254. 10 ptchs. £6. Eastr-Oct. 2m west of Devizes on A361; 0.5m East of jnctn A361 & A365. On site/nearby: toilets, shwrs, hook-ups, payphone, shop, pub rstrnts.

40. Thorney Lakes, Thorney Farm, Muchelney, Langport, Somerset, TA10 0DW. Richard & Ann England. 01458 250811. 16 ptchs. £6. Mar-Nov. 1m from Muchelney. On site/nearby: toilets, shwrs, hook-ups.

41. Lowtrow Cross Inn, Upton, Taunton, Somerset, TA4 2DB. Mrs MI Umney. 01398 371111/371220. 23 ptchs. £5-£7. Apr-Oct. From N, exit M5 jnctn 25, follow A358 to Cedar Falls, L B3224 to Upton. From S, exit M5 jnctn 27 to Bampton & continue on B3190 to Upton. On site/nearby: toilets, shwrs, hook-ups, laund fac, payphone, pub, rstrnt.

42. Southdown Farm, Brixham, Devon, TQ5 0AJ. S. Love. Tel/fax 01803 857991. 3/4 ptchs. £7.50-£10. May-Sept. If towing enter from Hillhead along Gattery Lane & farm track. If not come up (steep) Southdown Hill Road from Brixham. On site/nearby: toilets, shwrs.

43. Ashburton, Waterleat, Ashburton, TQ13 7HU. Mr Gordon Honor. 01364 652552. 35 ptchs. £4-£9. Eastr-Oct. From centre of Ashburton (off A38), R North Street; before bridge bear R; follow signs Waterleat/Camping 1.5m. On site/nearby: toilets, shwrs, hook-ups, laund fac, payphone, shop.

44. Bundu, Sourton Cross, Okehampton, Devon, EX20 4HT. LA & GB Strange. 01837 861611. 38 ptchs. £4-£6.50. 4m past Okehampton, slip road to to Tavistock A386. At jnctn turn L, 500 metres, L again. On site/nearby: toilets, shwrs, hook-ups, laund fac, payphone, shop, pub, rstrnt.

45. Barley Meadow, Crockernwell, Exeter, EX6 6NR. Meri & Geoff Cox. 01647 281629. 40 ptchs. £6.50-£7.50. Small tents £3 per person. mid-Mar – Oct.A30 from Exeter to Okehampton. 1st L to Cheriton Bishop/Crockernwell. 2.5m to site. On site/nearby: toilets, shwrs, disabled unit, hook-ups, laund fac, payphone, shop, pub, rstrnt.

46. Yeate Farm, Boddinick-by-Fowey, Cornwall, PL23 1LZ. Mrs A Oliver. 01726 870256. 30 ptchs. £5.50-£7.50. Eastr-Oct. Site is on R just before Bodinnick on minor road ldg from B3359. On site/nearby: toilets, shwrs, hook-ups, laund fac, meals, pub.

47. Tamar Lake Farm, Thurdon, Kilkhampton, Bude, Cornwall, EX23 9SA. Paul Woodhead. 01288 321426. 15 ptchs. £3.50-£4.50. Apr-Oct. From S side of Kilkhampton on A39 follow signs to Tamar Lakes. Ignore signs for Upper Tamar Lakes & continue 200 yds to farm on L. On site/nearby: toilets, shwrs.

48. Trevean Farm, St. Merryn, Padstow, Cornwall, Pl28 8PR. Mrs MJ Rayment. 01841 520772. 36 ptchs. From £5. Apr-Oct. From St Merryn village, take B3276 Newquay road for 1m, then turn L. Site 1st farm on R. On site/nearby: toilets, shwrs, hook-ups, laund fac, payphone, shop, pub, rstrnt.

49. Home Farm, Rectory Lane, Puncknowle, Nr Dorchester, Dorset, DT2 9BW. Miss R Laver. 01308 897258. 22 ptchs. From £3. Apr-Oct. From Dorchester: on A35 between Dorchester & Bridport turn off to Litton Cheney & follow road to Punknowle. From Bridport: take B3157 twds Weymouth, turn off at Bull Inn, Swyre. On site/nearby: toilets, shwrs, hook-ups, payphone, shop, pub meals.

50. Batcombe Vale, Shepton Mallet, Somerset, BA4 6BW. Donald Sage. Tel/fax 01749 830246; E.Mail 100421.3001@compuserve.com 32 ptchs. £7-£8. Eastr-Oct. Off B3081 between Bruton & Evercreech from where it is signed. On site/nearby: toilets, ch shwr block, hook-ups, payphone, meals, shop, pub.

51. Mendip Heights, Priddy, Nr Wells, Somerset, BA5 3BP. Ann & David Barnes. 01749 870241. 90 ptchs. £6.40-£7. Mar-mid Nov. From A38 take A371 to Cheddar, then B3135 to Priddy & follow signs. On site/nearby: toilets, shwrs, hook-ups, laund fac, payphone, shop, pub meals.

52. Dykegreen Farm, Clovelly, Bideford, Devon, EX39 5RY. J Johns. Tel 01237 431699; fax 01237 431689. 30 ptchs. From £6.50. Eastr-Oct. Site on A39 junction with Clovelly Road. On site/nearby: toilets, shwrs, hook-ups, payphone, shop, pub, rstrnt.

53. Fishponds House, Dunkeswell, Honiton, Devon, EX14 0SH. Rick Cattle. Tel 01404 891358; Fax 01404 891109. 15 ptchs. £5-£7. All year. Exit A303 Honiton. Follow signs to Luppitt & Smeatharpe. Fishponds Farm marked by RAC sign. 6.5m from Honiton. On site/nearby: toilets, shwrs, hook-ups, laund fac, payphone, pub, rstrnt.

54. Carbeil, Trelidon Lane, Downderry, Nr Torpoint, Cornwall. Mrs & Ms Stocker. 01503 250636. 20 ptchs. £5-£10.50. Eastr-Oct. From A387 turn S onto B3247 for Seaton & continue twds Downderry. Turn L at St Nicholas Church for site. On site/nearby: toilets, shwrs, hook-ups, laund fac, payphone, meals, shop, pub, rstrnt.

55. Ruthern Valley, Ruthernbridge, Bodmin, Cornwall, PL30 5LU. Brian & Chris Smith. 01208 831395/Freephone 0500 151610. 30 ptchs. £7.50-£9.30. Apr-Oct. Frm Bodmin take A391 twds St Austell. Turn R at 2nd Ruthernbridge sign. After 0.75m turn L & filter L again to Ruthernbridge (1m). Turn L before bridge, site is 300 yds on L. On site/nearby: toilets, shwrs, hook-ups, laund fac, payphone.

56. Bosavern House, St Just in Penwith, Penzance, Cornwall, TR19 7RD. Bob & Alison Hartley. 01736 788301. 12 ptchs. £5-£6. Mar-Oct. West of Penzance on B3306 between St Just and Sennen. On site/nearby: toilets, shwrs, hook-ups, laund fac, payphone, shop.

57. Troytown Farm, St. Agnes, Isles of Scilly, Cornwall, TR22 0PL. Mrs SJ Hicks. 01720 422360. £5.50-£6. Enquire for details, booking essential. On site/nearby: toilets, shwrs, laund fac, payphone, store, cafes, pub meals.

58. Seven Arches Farm, Chitts Hill, Lexdon, Colchester, Essex, CO5 5SX. Jill Tod. Tel/fax. 01206 574896. 5 ptchs. £6. From A12 turn N onto A604 W of Colchester, then 1st right, site 2m on R.
On site/nearby: toilets, shwrs, hook-ups, pub.

59. Grange Farm, Whittington, King's Lynn, PE33 9TF. 01366 500307. 25 ptchs. £5. Mar-Oct.
On N side of A134, Northwold-Stoke Ferry Road at junctn A134/B1106. 1m S of Stoke Ferry.
On site/nearby: toilets, shwrs.

60. Matapos, Main Street, Fleet Hargate, Lincolnshire, PE12 8LL. Mr & Mrs Fowler. 01406 422910. 45 ptchs. £6. mid Mar-mid Oct. 3m E of Holbeach on A17, on R at end of village just past Anglia Motel.
On site/nearby: toilets, shwrs, hook-ups, laund fac, payphone, shop, pub, rstrnt.

61. Brighthouse Farm, Melford Road, Lawshall, Nr Bury St Edmunds, Suffolk. Odell Truin. 01284 830385. 2 acre site. £3.50-£5.50. All Year. 8m S of Bury St Edmunds. Turn R off A134 to Lawshall. Thru' village, 1st left in 0.75m, at Xroads L into Melford Road. Farm 0.25m on left.
On site/nearby: toilets, shwrs, hook-ups, pub, rstrnt.

62. Honeypot, Wortham, Eye, Suffolk, IP22 1PW. Nicholas & Caroline Smith. Tel 01379 783312; fax 01379 783293. 35 ptchs. £5.50-£9.50. Apr-Sept. S of A143 Bury St Edmunds-Diss road, 4m SW of Diss in Wortham village.
On site/nearby: toilets, shwrs, hook-ups, laund fac, payphone, shop, pub, rstrnt.

63. Low House, Bucklesham Road, Foxhall, Ipswich, Suffolk, IP10 0AU. Mr John Booth. Tel 01473 659437; fax 01473 659880. 30 ptchs. £4.25-£6.50. All year.Turn off A14 Ipswich ring road (S) onto A1156 twds East Ipswich. In 1m turn R, in 0.5m turn R twds Bucklesham, site on L 0.25m.
On site/nearby: toilets, shwrs, hook-ups, laund fac, payphone, meals, pub.

64. Haveringland Hall, Cawston, Norwich, Norfolk, NR10 4PN. Richard Hinde. 01603 871302. £6-£8.50. Mar-Oct. From Norwich ring road turn N onto A140, then bear left onto B1149. At end of Horsford village bear left to Haveringland. Site 3m on R.
On site/nearby: toilets, shwrs, hook-ups.

65. Long Furlong Cottage, Blakeney-Saxlingham Road, Wiveton, Nr Holt, Norfolk, NR25 7DD. Mr Bennett, 01263 740833. Most of year. 34 ptchs. £4-£7. Mostly all year. From A148 Fakenham/Holt, turn L/R at Sharrington twds Langham B1156. At 2nd Xrds turn R onto 'By Road', 4th gateway on R.
On site/nearby: toilets, shwrs, hook-ups, laund fac, pub, rstrnt.

66. The Willows, Diss Road, Scole, Norfolk, IP21 4DH. Jean G Paull. 01379 740271. 32 ptchs. £6.50. May-Sept. 1.5m E of Diss, 200 yds off A140 Scole rndbt twds Diss.
On site/nearby: toilets, shwrs, hook-ups, laund fac, payphone, shop, pub, rstrnt.

67. Swans Harbour, Barford Road, Marlingford, Norwich, Norfolk, NR9 4BE. Mrs J Morter. 01603 759658. 30 ptchs. £5. All year. Take B1108 Norwich-Watton. 2.5m past Norwich southern by-pass, turn R at Xrds to Marlingford. Follow signs.
On site/nearby: toilets, shwrs, hook-ups, laund fac, payphone, shop, pub, rstrnt.

68. Road End Farm, Great Casterton, Stamford, Lincolnshire, PE9 4BB. C. Lamb. Tel 01780 63417; fax 01780 65656. 15 ptchs. £4. All year. Just off A1 London to North
On site/nearby: toilets, hook-ups, payphone, shop, pub, rstrnt.

69. Silver Birches, Waterside Road, Barton-on-Humber, N. Lincolnshire, DN18 5BA. Mrs J Wainwright. 01652 632509. 24 ptchs. £5.50. Apr-Oct. From A15 or A1077 follow Humber Bridge Viewing Area sign to Waterford Road. Site just past The Sloop pub.
On site/nearby: toilets, shwrs, hook-ups, laund fac, payphone, shop, pub, rstrnt.

70. Willlowmere, Bures Road, Little Cornard, Sudbury, Suffolk. Mrs A Wilson. 01787 375559. 40 ptchs. From £7. Eastr-Oct. 1.5m S of Sudbury on B1508 Bures road.
On site/nearby: toilets, shwrs, hook-ups, laund fac, shop, pub, rstrnt.

71. St Margaret's, Shottisham, Nr Woodbridge, Suffolk, IP12 3HD. Mr & Mrs Norton. 01394 411247. 25 ptchs. £5. Apr-Oct. 3m NE of Woodbridge at Wilford Bridge (A1152), turn S onto B1083 for 4m. Turn E thr' Shottisham for 0.5m.
On site/nearby: toilets, shwrs, hook-ups, payphone, pub meals.

72. Chestnut Farm, Gisleham, Nr. Lowestoft, Suffolk, NR33 8EE. Mr Neville Collen. 01502 740227. £5. Mar-Oct. At Kessingland S rndbt on A12, turn W for Gisleham, then 2nd left.
On site/nearby: toilets, shwrs, hookups, pub, rstrnt.

73. Thorpe Woodland, Santon Downham, Brandon, Suffolk, IP27 0TJ. Forest Enterprise. 01842 810271 or 01842 751042. 138 pitches. £4-£5. Apr-Dec. Take A1066 from Thetford. After 5m bear left to East Harling. Site 0.25m on left.
On site/nearby: hook-ups.

74. Whaplode Manor, Saracens Head, Holbeach, Lincolnshire, PE12 8AZ. Mrs S Wood. Tel 01406 422837; fax 01406 426824. 20 ptchs. Eastr-Nov. Just off A17 3m N of Holbeach.
On site/nearby: toilets, shwrs, hook-ups, laund fac, payphone, shop, bar, rstrnt.

75. Riverside, Wainfleet Bank, Wainfleet, Skegness. Mrs J Bingham. 01754 880205. 30 ptchs. £4.50-£5. Mid Mar-mid Oct. On A52 from Boston to Wainfleet, turn L onto B1195 twds Wainfleet All Saints. 150 yds after river bridge turn L at sign Wainfleet Bank. Site 1m.
On site/nearby: toilets, shwrs, hook-ups, laund fac.

76. Broadclose Farm, Inkberrow, Worcester, WR7 4JW. Mrs A Steel. 01386 792266. 10 ptchs. £3. All year.
Off A422 turn in village up Stone Pit Lane. Over Xrds to farm.
On site/nearby: toilets, shwrs, shop.

77. Dodwell Park, Evesham Road, Stratford-upon-Avon, Warwickshire, CV37 9ST. Mrs Shirley Bennett.
01789 204957. 50 ptchs. £4-£9. All year. 2m SW of Stratford on B439.
On site/nearby: toilets, shwrs, hook-ups, laund fac, payphone, shop, pub.

78. The Alamo, Kniveton Wood, Kniveton, Ashbourne, DE6 1JF. Mrs Martin. 01335 345731. 15 ptchs. From £4.
B5035 Ashbourne to Wirksworth, turn L to Kniveton Wood, past 2nd house take 2nd gate.
On site/nearby: toilets, washing fac, hook-ups, pub.

79. Mill Marina, Midland Road, Thrapston, Northamptonshire, NN14 4JR. Lionel Phillips. 01832 732850. 45 ptchs. Abt £9. Take Thrapston exit from A14 or A605, and follow signs.
On site/nearby: toilets, shwrs, hook-ups, laund fac, payphone, shop, pub, rstrnt.

80. Engine & Tender Inn, Nr Ludlow, Shropshire. Marie Rossler. 01588 660275. 30 ptchs. Abt £5. All year.
W from Craven Arms on B4368, fork left to B4367. Site in village on R in 2m.
On site/nearby: toilets, shwrs, hook-ups, payphone, pub, rstrnt.

81. Park House, Brimfield, Ludlow, Shropshire, SY8 4NY. Mr & Mrs D Forbes. 01584 711558. 6 ptchs. £5-£10. All year.
Midway between Ludlow & Leominster on A49. 2m S of Woofferton Xrds. 2 white milk churns mark site entrance.
On site/nearby: toilets, pub, rstrnt.

82. Small Batch, Little Stretton, Church Stretton, Shropshire, SY6 6PW. Mrs P R Prince. 01694 723358. 32 ptchs.
£6. Mid Apr-Sept. Off A49 into Little Stretton, onto B4370. L at Rogleth Inn. Site 0.25m on right.
On site/nearby: toilets, shwrs, shop, pub.

83. Park Grange, Morville, Bridgnorth, Shropshire, WV16 4RN. Mrs Carol Skinner. 01746 714285. 5 ptchs. All year.
On A458 midway between Bridgnorth & Much Wenlock.
On site/nearby: pub.

84. The Blount Arms, Forest Park, Cleobury Mortimer, Nr Kidderminster, Shropshire, DY14 9BE. Mr & Mrs L Bagley. 01299 270423. 32 ptchs. £5. Mar-Oct. 1.5m from Cleobury Mortimer on A4117.
On site/nearby: toilets, shwrs, hook-ups, payphone, shop, pub meals.

85. Kingsgreen, Berrow, Nr Great Malvern, Worcestershire, WR13 6AQ. Keith & Jill Davis. 01531 650272. 45 ptchs. £5-£6. Mar-Nov. From M50 J2, take A417 twds Gloucester for 1.5m, then L onto B4208 signed to Malverns.
On site/nearby: toilets, shwrs, hook-ups, payphone, disabled fac, shop, pub, rstrnt.

86. Glencote, Station Road, Cheddleton, Nr Leek, Staffordshire, ST13 7EE. Hilda Birch. Tel 01538 360745; fax 01538 361788. 60 ptchs. £7.80/. Apr-Oct. S from Leek on A520, at Cheddleton turn L at foot of hill along Station Road.
On site/nearby: toilets, shwrs, hook-ups, laund fac, payphone, shop, pub.

87. Mill Farm, Long Compton, Shipston on Stour, Warwickshire, CV36 5NX. Mr J H Salmon. 01608 684663. 11 ptchs. £5. Apr-Oct. Turn W off A3400 in Long Compton, for 0.5m, site on R.
On site/nearby: toilets, pub.

88. Sycamore, Lant Lane, Tansley, Derbyshire, DE4 5LF. Charles Boffey. 01629 55760. 60 ptchs. ú6-ú8. Mid Mar-mid Oct. From Chester-Matlock road (A632) turn twds Tansley, in 0.75m R to Chatsworth House, Riber Nature Reserve.
On site/nearby: toilets, shwrs, laund fac, hook ups, payphone, shop.

89. Park Farmhouse, Donington Park, Castle Donington, Derbyshire, DE74 2RN. J Shields. Tel 01332 862409; fax 01332 862364. 65 ptchs. £7-£12. All year. Adjacent competitors' entrance to Donington Park racecourse.
On site/nearby: toilets, shwrs, hook-ups, pub, rstrnt.

90. Haytop Country Park, Whatstandswell, Nr Matlock, Derbyshire, DE4 5HP. Mr H George. 01773 852063. All year.
M1 J28, take A38 twds Derby for 6m, then A610 to Ambergate. R onto A6 for 3m to Whatstandwell Bridge. Cross bridge, L onto layby & turn up drive.
On site/nearby: toilets, washing fac, payphone, pub, meals.

91. Woodland, Forest Enterprise Campsite Office, Coleford, Gloucestershire, GL16 7NW. 01594 833376. 90 ptchs.
£5-£9. Mar-Nov. From Monmouth take A4136 E to Christchurch. At Pike House Inn go N for 0.5m, following campsite signs. Reception is on L.
On site/nearby: hook-ups, shop.

92. Hogsdown Farm, Lower Wick, Dursley, Gloucestershire, GL11 6DS. Jenny Smith. 01453 810224. 20 ptchs. £6-£8.50. All year. Off A38 between J 13 & 14.
On site/nearby: toilets, shwrs, hook-ups, laund fac, payphone, pub.

93. Lower Ruxton Farm, Kings Caple, Herefordshire, HR1 4TX. Mr H D Jenkins. 01432 840223. 20 ptchs. £2-£5.
E of A49 between Ross-on-Wye/Hereford. Follow signs to Kings Caple, cross river bridge, turn R to Ruxton.
On site/nearby: pub.

94. Springs Farm, Lothersdale, Nr. Skipton, Yorkshire. Mrs H Cotterill. Tel 01535 632533; fax 01756 799848. 30 ptchs. £6.50-£8. Apr-Nov. From Crosshills S of Skipton on A629, follow c'van signs to Lothersdale.
On site/nearby: toilets, shwrs, hook-ups, payphone, shop, pub.

95. Shaw Ghyll, Simonstone, Hawes, N Yorkshire, DL8 3LY. Mr Roger Stott. Tel 01969 667359; fax 01969 667894. 30 ptchs. 2m N of Hawes on Muker road.
On site/nearby: toilets, shwrs, hook-ups, laund fac, payphone, shop, pub, rstrnt.

96. Howgill Lodge, Barden, Skipton, N. Yorkshire, BD23 6DJ. Bernard & Ann Foster. 01756 720655. 30 ptchs. £8-£8.50. End Mar-Oct. From Bolton Abbey on A59 take B6160 twds Burnsall. At Barden Tower (3.5m) turn R twds Appletreewick for 1.5m. Turn R into lane by tel box & sign.
On site/nearby: toilets, shwrs, hook-ups, laund fac, payphone, shop, rstrnt.

97. Earth's Wood, Bank End Lane, Barnsley Road, Clayton West, Huddersfield, HD8 9LJ. Mr & Mrs J Auckland. Tel 01484 863211/864266; fax 01484 863820. 40 ptchs. From £5.50. Mar-Oct. Turn off A636 opp Junction Inn. Follow rd thr' Clayton West twds High Hoyland for 1m. Site on R 80 yds past S Yorkshire sign.
On site/nearby: toilets, shwrs, hook-ups, laund fac.

98. Stubbings Farm, Leeds Road, Otley, LS21 1DN. Mr Rimmer. 01943 464168. 1.5 acres. £4. All year. 1m E of Otley off A660, opp small lay-by.
On site/nearby: toilets, laund fac, pub, rstrnt.

99. Usha Gap, Muker, Richmond, N Yorkshire, DL11 6DW, Mrs Metcalfe. 01748 886214. £7; £2.50 tents. All year. From Richmond take B6270. Site between Muker & Thwaite.
On site/nearby: toilets, shwrs, hook-ups, laund fac, shop, pub, rstrnt.

100. West Roods Working Farm, Boldron, Barnard Castle, County Durham, DL12 9SW. Mrs Margaret Lowson. 01833 690116. 16 ptchs. From £6. Apr-Oct. 2m S of Barnard Castle. Entrance to site from N side of A66, 2.5m E of Bowes, 0.5 W of road to Boldron village. 1st R, 1st L to entrance.
On site/nearby: toilets, shwrs, hook-ups, laund fac, payphone, rstrnt.

101. Proctor Steads, Craster, Alnwick, Northumberland, NE66 3TF. Robert W Davidson. 01665 576613. 60 ptchs. From £7. Mar-Oct. From A1 at Alnwick take B1340 for 3m, follow signs to site.
On site/nearby: toilets, shwrs, hook-ups, laund fac, payphone, shop, pub, meals, rstrnt.

102. Demesne Farm, Bellingham, Hexham, Northumberland, NE48 2BS. T & K Telfer. 01434 220258. 30 ptchs. From £5; £2 tent. All year. Centre of Bellingham just off B6320 on W Woodburn road.
On site/nearby: toilets, shwrs, hook-ups, laund fac, payphone, shop, pub, rstrnt.

103. Mill Farm Country Park, Mill Lane, Skipsea, Driffield, E Yorkshire, YO25 8SS. Judy Willmott. 01262 468211. 35 ptchs. £4-£6.85. Mar-mid Oct. On A165 Hull to Bridlington, at Beeford take B1249 to Skipsea, at Xrds turn R, then 1st L up Cross Street to Mill Lane.
On site/nearby: toilets, shwrs, hook-ups, laundry fac, payphone, shop, pub, meals.

104. Hollins Farm, Glaisdale, Whitby, Yorkshire, YO21 2PZ. Mr & Mrs Mortimer. 01947 897516. 20 ptchs. £1.50 per person. All year. Glaisdale is 4m from A171. site 1m up valley from village.
On site/nearby: toilets, shwrs, shop, pub.

105. Riverside, Ferry Lane, Bishopthorpe, York, YO2 1SB. D A Smith. Tel 01904 704442/705812; fax 01904 705824. 25 ptchs. £7.50-£9. Eastr-Sept. Bishopthorpe is 2m S of York off A1036.
On site/nearby: toilets, shwrs, hook-ups, laund fac, payphone, shop, rstrnt.

106. Viewly Hill, Tow Law, Bishop Auckland, Co. Durham, DL13 4HH. Mrs Hodgson. 01388 730308. 5 ptchs. On A68 1m NE of Tow Law turn onto B6296 to Walsingham. Site 0.5m on R.
On site/nearby: toilets. At 2m: shop, pub, rstrnt.

107. Rowter Farm, Castleton, Nr Sheffield, S30 2WA. Mrs B Hall. 01433 620271. 50 ptchs. Eastr-Oct. 2.5m from Castleton. Take Winnatts Pass Road to B6061, cont straight on for 200 yds, turn L thr' white gate.
On site/nearby: toilets, washing fac.

108. Kielder, Earls Burn, Bellingham, Nr Hexham, Northumberland, NE48 2AJ. Forest Enterprise. 01434 250291 when open; 01434 220242 other times. 70 ptchs. £5-£9. Apr-Sept. 500 yds N of Kielder village on R.
On site/nearby: toilets, shwrs, hook-ups, laund fac, payphone, shop, disabled fac.

109. Low Whita Farm, Low Row, Richmond, N Yorkshire, DL11 6NT. Mrs S Clarkson. 01748 884430. From £2. On B6270 12m to E of Richmond. At farmhouse: toilet, h & c water.

110. Nostell Priory, Nostell, Wakefield, West Yorkshire, WF4 1QD. Mrs Sylvia White. 01924 863938. 60 ptchs. £7.50-£8.50. End Mar-Sept. Off A638 Wakefield-Doncaster road, 5m from Wakefield.
On site/nearby: toilets, shwrs, hook-ups, laund fac, payphone.

111. Ashcroft Farm, Bardon Mill, Hexham, Northumberland, NE47 7JA. Mrs J Robson. 01434 344409. 5 ptchs. £3.50. Apr-Oct. 5m E of Haltwhistle turn off A69 into Bardon Mill village. 1st L then R.
On site/nearby: payphone, pub.

112. Cottage Farkm, Blackwell in the Peak, Buxton, Derbyshire, SK17 9QT. Mrs M Gregory. 01298 85330. 30 ptchs. From £6. Mar-Oct. Midway between Buxton & Bakewell off A6.
On site/nearby: toilets, shwrs, hook-ups, payphone, shop.

113. The Grouse & Claret, Rowley, Matlock, Derbyshire, DE4 2EL. John Miley. 01629 733233. 29 ptchs. £7.50. All year. On A6 betwen Bakewell & Matlock.
On site/nearby: toilets, shwrs, hook-ups, payphone, pub meals.

114. Laundsfield, Stoney Lane, Galgate, Nr Lancaster. Mrs A Close. 01524 751313. 10 ptchs. £4. All year. M6 J33, turn R onto A6 (Lancaster), 1st R at traffic lights in Galgate. Site 100 yds on R.
On site/nearby: toilets, meals, shop, pub.

115. Camelot, Longtown Carlisle, Cumbria, CA6 5SZ. Eric & Monica Lee. 01228 791248. 20 ptchs. £6.70; tents £3-£5.70. 4m from J44 M & 1m S of Longtown on A7.
On site/nearby: toilets, shwrs, hook-ups, laund fac, payphone, shop, pub.

116. Hawkrigg Farm, Colby, Appleby, Cumbria, CA16 6BB. Audrey Atkinson. 01768 351046 15 ptchs. £2-£3. From Appleby take B6260, turn R to Colby where turn L twds Kings Meaburn, then 1st R to site.
On site/nearby: toilets, shwrs, hook-ups, laund fac, payphone, shop, pub, rstrnt.

117. Burns Farm, St Johns-in-the-Vale, Keswick, Cumbria, CA12 4RR. Mrs L Lamb. 017687 79225. 37 ptchs. £5-£7.50. Seasonal. S of A66 just W of Keswick on minor road. Follow signs to Ancient Stone Circle.
On site/nearby: toilets, shwrs, payphone.

118. Gill Head, Troutbeck, Penrith, Cubria CA11 0ST. J Wilson. 01768 779652. 40 ptchs. £3.50-£10. Mar-Nov. From A66 Penrith/Keswick road turn S onto A5091. In 100 yds turn R. Site 0.5m on R.
On site/nearby: toilets, shwrs, hook-ups, laund fac, payphone.

119. Violet Bank, Simonscales Lane, Cockermouth, Cumbria, CA13 9TG. John Harrold. 01900 822169. 30 ptchs. £4.90-£6.40. Mar-mid Nov. Leave Cockermouth centre via Lorton Road (B5292). After 0.25m turn R into Vicarage Lane ldg on to Simonscales Lane, then on to country lane.
On site/nearby: toilets, shwrs, hook-ups, laund fac, payphone, shop.

120. Pier Cottage, Coniston, Cumbria, LA21 8AJ. A & I Wilson. 015394 41497. 10 ptchs. £7.50. Mar-Oct. From Coniston take road twds Hawkshead B5285 & over hump-back bridge. After 300 yds turn R over cattle grid, follow unmade road twds lake.
On site/nearby: toilets, shwrs, hook-ups, shop, pub, rstrnt.

121. Fisherground Farm, Eskdale, Cumbria, CA19 1TF. Ian Hall. 01946 723319. 100 ptchs. £7-£9. Mar-Nov. From M6 J36, follow A590 & A595 to Broughton-in-Furness. 0.75m after Broughton turn R to Ulpha. Turn L in Ulpha to Eskdale. Follow fell road to King George IV pub (6m). Turn R, 1st L.
On site/nearby: toilets, shwrs, hook-ups, laund fac, payphone, shop, pub, rstrnt.

122. High Laning Farm, Dent, Cumbria. Margaret Taylor. 015396 25239. 73 ptchs. £3 per person. All year. M6 J37. A684 to Sedburgh, signed to Dent.
On site/nearby: toilets, shwrs, hook-ups, laund fac, payphone, shop, pub, rstrnt.

123. Oakbank Lakes, Longtown, Carlisle, Cumbria, CA6 5NA. Mike Powell. Tel/fax 01228 791108. 20 ptchs. All year. Just N of Longtown off A7.
On site/nearby: toilets, shwrs, hook-ups, snacks.

124. Strawberry Wood, Farm Lane, Lower Withington, Macclesfield, Cheshire, SK11 9DU. Paul Jenkinson. 01477 571407. 25 ptchs. Mar-Oct. From M6 J18 take A54 to Holmes Chapel, then A535 Macclesfield road for 4m. Turn R into Farm Lane (B5392). Site 700 yds on R.
On site/nearby: toilets, shwrs, hook-ups, laund fac, shop.

125. Gathurst Hall Farm, Shevington, Wigan, Lancashire, WN6 8JA. Mrs Helen Smith. 01257 253464. 25 ptchs. £5. Apr-Oct. M6 J26: Orrell, B5026 Shevington; M6 J27: B5029 Standish, B5026 Shevington.
On site/nearby: toilets, shwrs, hook-ups, payphone, shop, pub, rstrnt.

126. Northwood Hall, Kelsall, Chester, Cheshire. Mr & Mrs A Knock. 01829 752569. 30 ptchs. £6.50-£8. All year. Off A54 7m E of Chester in Kelsall – M6 J18.
On site/nearby: toilets, shwrs, hook-ups, laund fac, shop.

127. Bayesbrown Farm, Great Langdale, Ambleside, Cumbria, LA22 9JZ. Mr & Mrs D Rowland. 015394 37300. 6 ptchs for caravans, many more for tents. £4.60. From Ambleside take A593 to Skelwith Bridge, then B5343 to Chapel Stile. Site up track to L.
On site/nearby: toilets, washing fac, breakfast, pub meals.

128. Birchbank, Blawith, Ulverston, Cumbria, LA12 8EW. Mrs L Niclolson, 01229 885277. 5 ptchs. From £3.50. May-Oct. On A5092, 0.5m W of Gawthwaite. Turn for Woodland (over cattle grid). Site 1.7m on R.
On site/nearby: toilets, washing fac, hook-ups, laund fac.

129. Melbreak, Carr lane, Middleton, Lancashire, LA3 3LH. AE & GA Syson. 01524 852430. 2 acres. £6.30. M6 J34. Follow A683 past Lancaster to Heysham Docks. Turn L at rndbt to Middleton, then R to site.
On site/nearby: toilets, shwrs, laund fac, shop, snacks.

Reference Section Wales

130. Afan Argoed, Afan Forest Park, Cynonville, Port Talbot, West Galmorgan, SA13 3HG. Information Desk. 01639 850564. 10 ptchs. Apr-Oct. M4 J40. A4107 NE for 6m to Countryside Centre.
On site/nearby: toilets, payphone, shop, pub, rstrnt.
131. Glydach Gorge, Station Road, Clyddach, Gilwern, Monmouthshire, NP7 0RD. Susan Doherty, Monmouthsire C.C.. Tel 01633 644844; fax 01633 644800. 25 ptchs. £5. Seasonal. Off the A465 Heads of the Valleys Road between Abergavenny & Ebbw Vale. On site/nearby: toilets, shwrs, hook-ups, shop, pub, rstrnt.
132. Grawen Farm, Cwm-Taf, Cefn Coed, Merthyr Tydfil, Mid Glamorgan. F. Pugh. 01685 723740. Apr-Oct. Alongside A470 Brcon Beacons road, 2m from Cefn Coed. On site/nearby: toilets, shwrs, hook-ups, laund fac.
133. Pencelli Castle, Pencelli, Brecon, Powys, LD3 7LX. Gerwyn & Liz Rees. 01874 665451. 20 ptchs. £7.50; £3.50 tents. A40 E from Brecon for 2m. Turn onto B4558 twds Llanfrynach & go S thr' Pencelli. On leaving village, site is on L.
On site/nearby: toilets, shwrs, hook-ups, laund fac, payphone, shop, pub.
134. Cross Inn & Black Mountain, Llanddeusant, Llangadog, Dyfed, Carmarthenshire, SA19 9YG. Walter Smith. 01550 740621. 25 ptchs. £4-£6. All year. Nr Llangadog, just off A40 between Llandovery & Llandeilo.
On site/nearby: toilets, shwrs, hook-ups, laund fac, payphone, pub, rstrnt.
135. Coedirion, Llanddarog, Carmarthenshire, SA32 8BH. Selwyn & Daphne Evans. 01267 275666. 20 ptchs. £6-£8. Mar-Xmas. 500 metres from A48, 6m E of Carmarthen at Llanddarog.
On site/nearby: toilets, shwrs, hook-ups, payphone, shop, pub, rstrnt.
136. Mount Pleasant, Penffordd, Nr Narberth, Pembrokeshire, SA66 7HY. Mrs Pauline Bowen.01437 563447. 5 c'vans + tents. £4.50. All year. Turn N off A40 at Redstone Cross onto B4313 twds Fishguard. After 3.5m, approaching Gelli, continue straight on minor road, over bridge & turn R under railway bridge to Penfford. Turn R in village. Site just past tel box. On site/nearby: toilets, shwrs, hook-ups, payphone.
137. St Davids Farm Park, St Davids, Pembrokeshire, SA62 6PH. David & Margaret Jarvis. 01437 721601. 6 acres. All year. Take Porthclais road out of St Davids via harbour, farm signed. On site/nearby: toilets, shwrs.
138. Dolbryn, Capel Iwan Road, Newcastle Emlyn, Carmarthneshire, SA38 9LP. Maureen & Brian Gent. 01239 710683. 40 ptchs. £4. Eastr-Oct. Turn S off A484 in Newcastle Emlyn past Leisure Centre, follow camping signs along Capel Iwan Road. On site/nearby: toilets, shwrs, hook-ups, bar.
139. Tycanol, Newport, Pembrokeshire, SA42 0ST. Mr Hugh Harries. 01239 820264. 30 ptchs. £6. All year. E of Fishguard, 500 yds NW of A487, 1m W of Newport. On site/nearby: toilets, shwrs, hook-ups.
140. Fforest Fields, Hundred House, Builth Wells, Powys. GT Barstow. 01982 570406. 40 ptchs. £7; £3 tents. 4m from Builth Wells on A481. On site/nearby: toilets, shwrs, hook-ups, laund fac, payphone, shop, pub, rstrnt.
141. Tan-yr-allt Farm, Ciliau-Aeron, Lampeter, Dyfed, SA48 8BU. Mr & Mrs Daniel Davies. 01570 470211. 3 acres. All year. On A482 in Ciliau-Aeron, 4m SW of Aberaeron. On site/nearby: toilets.
142. Pantmawr, Pisgah, Capel Seion, Aberystwyth, Dyfed, SY23 4NF. Mr & Mrs John Griffiths. 01970 880449. 25 ptchs. £3. Eastr-Oct. On A4120 Aberystwyth/Devil's Bridge road. 3.5m W of Devil's Bridge.
On site/nearby: toilets, washing fac, pub rstrnt.
143. Cringoed, Llanbrynmair, Powys, SY19 7DR. Mrs B Cornwall. 01650 521237. 40 ptchs. £6. Eastr-Oct.
On A470 Newtown/Machynlleth road, turn S onto B4518 at Llanbrynmair. Site 1m on R.
On site/nearby: toilets, shwrs, hook-ups, laund fac, payphone, meals, shop, pub.
144. Doleinion, Talyllyn, Tywyn, Gwnedd, LL36 9AJ. Marian Rees. 01654 761312. 35 ptchs. £2.50-£8.
NE of Tywyn on B4405 300 yds from jnctn with A487. On site/nearby: toilets, shwrs, hook-ups, pub, rstrnt.
145. Gesail Farm, Bryncrug, Tywyn, Gwynedd, LL36 9TL. Mrs Wendy Jones. 01654 782286. 20 ptchs. £4. Eastr-Oct. From A487 to Machynlleth, turn on to B4405 twds Tywyn for 3m. Turn R onto minor road for Llanegryn. At signpost turn L for Bryncrug & Llanegryn. Continue for 2m past Bird-Rock. Site is next on L.
On site/nearby: toilets, shwrs, payphone, meals, shop, pub.
146. Tynbryn, Llanfihangel, Tywyn, Gwynedd, LL36 9TN. Mrs Mary Jones. 01654 782277. 9 ptchs. Mar-Oct. At Abergynolwyn on B4405 turn W twds Llanegryn for 1.5m. At tel box turn L for LLanegryn. Site 0.5m on L from Xrds. On site/nearby: toilets, shwrs, laund fac, pub.
147. Bryn Gwyn Farm, Llanuwchllyn, Bala, Gwynedd, LL23 7UB. Mrs MA Roberts. 01678 540687. 8 c'vans + tents. £8. Eastr-Nov. Site is 0.5m off A494 Bala/Dolgellau road, on Trawsfynedd mountain road, abt 1m from S end of Bala Lake. On site/nearby: toilets, shwrs, hook-ups, payphone, pub meals.
148. Glan Ceirw, Tynant, Nr Corwen, Clwyd, LL21 0RF. R Clive Passant. 01490 420346. 9 ptchs. £6-7. Mar-Oct. Midway between Corwen & Betwys y Coed just off A5 twds Llangum. Site signed.
On site/nearby: toilets, shwrs, hook-ups, laund fac, payphone, shop, pub, rstrnt.
149. Cae Du, Beddgelert, Gwynedd, LL55 4NE. Mr T Johnson-Porter. 01766 890345. 35 ptchs. £6. All year.
Hdg NE from Beddgelert on A498, turn R in 150 yds. Site on R. On site/nearby: toilets, shwrs, payphone, shop, pub, rstrnt.
150. Llwyn-Bugeilydd Farm, Criccieth, Gwynedd, LL52 0PN. Robert Roberts. 01766 522235. 20 c'vans + tents. Apr-Oct. From Criccieth turn off A497 onto B4411. Site on R 1m.
On site/nearby: toilets, shwrs, hook-ups, laund fac, payphone, shop, pub, rstrnt.
151. Tyn Rhos Farm, Saron, Llanwnda, Caernarfon, Gwynedd, LL54 5UH. Mr WC & Mrs MJ Evans. 01286 830362, 20 ptchs. £5-£7. Mar-Oct. Turn off A487 Caernarfon to Portmadoc road after crossing bridge 0.5m at signpost Llanfaglan Saron. In 3m at R bend cont thr' gate to site.
On site/nearby: toilets, shwrs, hook-ups, laund fac, payphone, pub, rstrnt.
152. Greenacres Farm Park, Mancot, Deeside, Flintshire. Hilary Johnson. Tel/fax 01244 531147. 40 ptchs. £12. Eastr-Sept. Farm Park signed from Queensferry rndbt on A550 W of Chester.
On site/nearby: toilets, shwrs, hook-ups, payphone, shop, pub, rstrnt.
153. Garnedd, Lon Brynmair, Brynteg, Anglesey, LL78 8QA. Mrs M Bean. 01248 853240. 15 ptchs. £6. Eastr-Oct. From mainland cross Britannia (A5) or Menai Bridge. Then A5025 (Amlych/Benllech) thr' Pentraeth, L at end of layby with AA phone. In 2m L at T junctn. 100 yds L. Site 0.5m R.
On site/nearby: toilets, shwrs, hook-ups, laund fac, payphone, shop, pub, rstrnt.

154. Castle Point, Rockcliffe, By Dalbeattie, Galloway, DG5 4QL. Mr Bigham. 01556 630248 (when open) 01241 860433 (when closed). 37 ptchs. £7-£9. Apr-Oct. From Dalbeattie take A710 coastal road. After 5m turn R to Rockcliffe. Site at brow of hill. On site/nearby: toilets, shwrs, laund fac, hook-ups, payphone, shop, pub, rstrnt.
155. Whitecairn Farm, Glenluce, Wigtownshire, DG8 0NZ. Mrs. Rankin. Tel/fax 01581 300267. 10 ptchs. £7-£9. Mar-Oct.1.5m N of Glenluce off A75. Follow signs to Motor Museum. Site 1m.
On site/nearby: toilets, washing fac, laund fac, hook-ups, payphone, shop, pub, rstrnt.
156. Barnsoul Farm, Irongray, Dumfries, DG2 95Q. A.J. Wight. Tel/fax 01387 730249. 20 ptchs. £6-£8. Apr-Oct. Just N of Dumfries on A76. On site/nearby: toilets, shwrs, laund fac, hook-ups, payphone, meals, pubs.
157. Mains Farm, Thornhill, Stirling, FK8 3QR. George and Mary Steedman. 01786 850605. 35 ptchs. £6-£7.50. Apr-Oct. From M9 exit 10 take A84. After 6m bear L onto A873. After 3m at Xrds in village L onto B822. Site in 125 metres. On site/nearby: toilets, shwrs, hook-ups, payphone, shop, pub, rstrnt.
158. Skeldon, Hollybush, nr. Ayre, KA6 7EB. T.H. Crossley, 01292 560502. 20 ptchs. Tents £4-£6.50. C/vans £7.50. Motor homes £8.50. May-Sept. Take A713 to Hollybush. Follow signs. On site/nearby: toilets, shwrs, hook-ups, payphone, shop, pub, rstrnt.
159. Newhouse, Ravenstruther, Lanark, ML11 8NP. J & M Seed. 01555 870228. 45 ptchs. £3-£7. mid-Mar-mid Oct. On A70 approx 45 mins drive from Glasgow & Edinburgh.
On site/nearby: toilets, shwrs, laund fac, hook-ups, payphone, shop, pub, rstrnt.
160. Woodland Gardens, Lundin links, Fife, KY8 5QG. Marjorie & Barry Nield. 01333 360319. 20 ptchs. £6.60-£11. Apr-Oct. Turn N off A915 (Kirkaldy-Leven-St. Andrews road) at E end of Lundin Links. Site is 0.5m from main road. On site/nearby: toilets, shwrs, laund fac, hook-ups, payphone, shop, pub, rstrnt.
161. Balquidder Braes, Balquidder Station, Lockhearnear, Perthshire, FK19 8NX. Mrs Eileen Fashae. Tel 01567 830293; fax 01567 830363. 25 ptchs. £6.50-£7.50. Eastr to Oct. From Lachearnhear take A84 twds Callander for 1.5m. Site entrance on L. On site/nearby: toilets, shwrs, laund fac, hook-ups, payphone, shop, pub, rstrnt.
162. Nether Craig, by Alyth, Blairgowrie, Perthshire, PH11 8HN. Mrs. June Nicoll. Tel 01575 560204; fax 01575 560315. 40 ptchs. £7-£9. Tents £2.50 per person. mid Mar – end Oct. At rndbt S of Alyth, join B954 signed Glenisla. Follow c'van signs for 4m. Do not go into Alyth.
On site/nearby: toilets, washing fac, shwrs, disabled fac, laund fac, hook-ups, payphone, shop, pub, rstrnt.
163. Arduaine Park, Arduaine, by Kilmelford, Argyll, PA34 4XA. John & Jane Rentoul. Tel 01852 200331; fax 01852 200337. 40 ptchs. £7-£10.50; small tents £3.25-£7.30. Mar-Oct. Take A816 S from Oban to Kilmelford. Site is signed to the R, between road and sea. On site/nearby: toilets, washing fac, shwrs, hook-ups, payphone, pub, rstrnt.
164. Oban Divers, Glenshellach, Oban, Argyll, PA34 4QJ. David Tye. Tel & fax 01631 562755. 50 ptchs. £6-£7. Mar-Nov. From N: A85 thr' Oban to traffic island following camp/car & ferry signs. Past Police Stn on L, then 1st L, 1st R & 1st L – signed to Glenshellach C & C Park . From S: thr' Oban to traffic island then L and as above.
On site/nearby: toilets, shwrs, laund fac, hook-ups, payphone, shop, pub, rstrnt.
165. Fiunary, Morvern, Argyll, PA34 5XX. Philip & Joanne Henderson. 01967 421225. 25 ptchs. £6.50-£7 May-Sept. Head N on A82 twds Fort William. Turn L at Corran Ferry sign (9m before Ft William). Follow signs to Lochaline. Site signed from there. On site/nearby: toilets, shwrs, hook-ups, payphone, meals, shop, pub.
166. Red Squirrel, Glencoe, Argyll, PA39 4HX. Mr. MacColl or Kathleen Grant. 01855 811256. 20 acres. £3.50. All year. The old Glencoe road near YHA. On site/nearby: toilets, shwrs, payphone, shop, pub, rstrnt.
167. Newdale, Tobermory, Isle of Mull, Argyll, PA75 6QF. Mrs Helen Williams. Tel/fax 01688 302306. 1.5 acres. 1.5m outside Tobemory on B8073 to Dervaig. On site/nearby: toilets, shwrs, shop, pub, rstrnt.
168. Garden House, Isle of Coll, Argyll, Inner Hebrides, PA78 6TB. Mr & Mrs K Graham. 01879 230374. 20 ptchs. £2 for tent, £5 for c'van for any time, then £2 per person per night. All year. Advance booking essential.
From Arinagour, turn L onto B8070. After 4m on L between Uig Cottage and Heather View, take track down to walled garden. NB: no petrol on island. On site/nearby: toilets, shwrs.
169. Portnarodoran, Airisaig, Inverness-shire. A & I MacDonald. Tel/fax 01687 450267. 30 ptchs. £5-£8.50. Apr-Oct. Approx. 2m N of Arisaig village. On site/nearby: toilets, shwrs, laund fac, hook-ups, payphone, shop, pub.
170. Dalraddy, by Aviemore, Inverness-shire, PH22 1QB. Tel 01479 810330; fax 01540 651380. ptchs. £6.50-£8; small tents £3-£4.50. All year except Nov.. Turn off A9 at Aviemore junction; at once R onto B9152; Park 2.5 miles on L. On site/nearby: toilets, shwrs, laund fac, hook-ups, shop.
171. Borlum Farm, Drumnadrochit, Inverness-shire, IV3 6XN. A.D. MacDonald-Haig. Tel 01456 450220; fax 01456 450358. 25 ptchs. £4-£8. All year. On the banks of Loch Ness, on the R just past Lewiston on the A82 heading from Inverness to Fort William. On site/nearby: toilets, shwrs, laund fac, hook-ups, payphone, shop, pub, rstrnt.
172. Spindrift, Little Kildrummie, Nairn, IV12 5QU. Mrs Sue Guillot. 01667 453992. 40 ptchs. £5.50-£8.50. Apr-Oct. From Nairn take B9090 Nairn/Cawdor road S for 1.5 m. Turn R at sharp L hand bend signed Little Kildrummie. Site 400 yards on L. On site/nearby: toilets, shwrs, laund fac, hook-ups, payphone, shop, pub, rstrnt.
173. Balmacara, Kyle of Lochalsh, West Highlands. Forest Enterprise. 01599 566 321. 55 ptchs. £4-£5. Small tents £2-£2.50. Apr-Sept. From E on A87 take 2nd road on R after Reraig village. On site/nearby: toilets, hook-ups.
174. Stroma View, Huna, John O'Groats, Wick Caithness. E & R Dundas. 01955 611313. 15 ptchs. From £5.50. Mar-Oct. Follow A9 to John O'Groats and turn L at Sea View Hotel. Follow A836 Thurso road for 1.5m. Site on L opp Isle of Stroma. On site/nearby: toilets, shwrs, laund fac, hook-ups.
175. Oldshoremore, by Lairg, Sutherland, IV27 4RS. J Mackenzie. 01971 521281. 15 ptchs. £5.30-£7.
Take A838 to Rhiconich; there join B801 to Kinlochbervie (4m) where take unclassified road to Oldshoremore (2m). On site/nearby: toilets, shwrs, hook-ups, shop, rstrnt.
176. Eilean Fraoich, North Shawbost, Isle of Lewis, HS2 9BQ. Iain Macaulay. 01851 710504. 20 ptchs. £7.50. Apr-Oct. On A858, 12m NW of Stornoway. On site/nearby: toilets, shwrs, laund fac, hook-ups, payphone, shop, pub, rstrnt.
177. Point of Ness, Ness Road, Stromness. Orkney Islands Council. Tel 01856 873535; fax 01856 876327. 20 ptchs. £2.50-£6. May-Sept. One mile west of the pierhead.
On site/nearby: toilets, shwrs, laund fac, hook-ups, payphone, pub, rstrnt.

Reference Section Ireland

178. Boatstrand, Dunabrattin, Annestown, Co. Waterford, Eire. Heather & Bruce MacDonald. 051 396110. 2 acres. £6. Mar-Nov. From Waterford, E on R675 (T63) thr' Tramore and along coast road to Annestown. At Boatstrand look for yellow thatched cottage and Woodcraft shop. On site/nearby: toilets, shwrs, shop, pub, rstrnt.
179. Glensheland Forest, Cappoquin, Co. Waterford, Eire. Eleanor Bell. Tel 058 60419; fax 058 60435. £5.50-£8.50. From Rosslare: M25 to Dungarvan, then N72 6m to Cappoquinn. Turn R to Glensheland Riverwalk (signed from Dungarvan). On site/nearby: toilets, shwrs, laund fac, hook-ups, payphone.
180. Jasmine Villa, Carrigtwohill, Co. Cork, Eire. Bill & Joe McGrath. 021 883234. 19 ptchs. £4-£7. All year. Site is on N25 Cork/Waterford/Rosslare road, 1.5km from Carrigtwhohill. On site/nearby: toilets, shwrs, hook-ups, campers' kitchen.
181. Blarney, Stone View, Blarney, Co. Cork, Eire. Mr. D. Quill. 021 385167. 40 ptchs. £8-£9. All year.
Take N20 from Cork, then R617 to Blarney. Site signed from Esso station.
On site/nearby: toilets, shwrs, laund fac, hook-ups, payphone, pubs, shop, rstrnts.
182. Creveen Lodge, Healy Pass Road, Lauragh, Co. Kerry, Eire. Mrs Mary Moriarty. 064 83131. 20 ptchs. £3-£7. Eastr-Oct. R at Soundbridge, Castletownbere Road R571 to Lauragh. L onto Healy Pass Road R574. Follow signs.
On site/nearby: toilets, shwrs, laund fac, hook-ups, payphone, pubs.
183. Wave Crest, Caherdanial, Ring of Kerry, Co. Kerry, Eire. Patrica Shaw Shea. Tel/fax 066 75188. 33 ptchs. £6-7. Small tents £2. mid-Mar-mid Oct. Site on main Ring of Kerry Road, 1.6km from Cahirdaniel.
On site/nearby: toilets, shwrs, laund fac, hook-ups, payphone, rstrnts, pubs.
184. Nore Valley, Bennettsbridge, Co. Kilkenny, Eire. Isobel Harper. Tel/fax 056 27229. 60 ptchs. £5-10. Mar-Oct. 11km S of Kilkenny. Turn R off B700 at Bennettsbridge.
On site/nearby: toilets, shwrs, laund fac, hook-ups, payphone, shop, rstrnt.
185. The Apple, Moorstown, Cahir, Co. Tipperary, Eire. Cornelius Traas. Tel 052 41459, Fax 052 42774. 32 ptchs. £3-£3.50 per adult. May-Sept. Between Clonmel (9km) and Cahir (6km) on main Waterford/Limerick road N24.
On site/nearby: toilets, shwrs, laund fac, hook-ups.
186. Green Acres, Aughacasla, Castlegregory, Co. Kerry, Eire. Thomas Keane. 066 39158. 40 ptchs. £5-£8. Eastr – Nov. 12m from Tralee on coast road to Connor Pass. Turn to beach in Aughacasla.
On site/nearby: toilets, shwrs, laund fac, hook-ups, payphone, shop, pub, rstrnt.
187. Aylevarroo, Kilrush, Co. Clare, Eire. Mary O'Gorman. 065 51102. 46 ptchs. £7-£8 mid-May-mid Sept.
On N side of River Shannon, 4m from Clare terminus of car ferry at Killimer.
On site/nearby: toilets, shwrs, laund fac, hook-ups, payphone, meals.
188. Moat Farm, Donard, Co. Wicklow, Eire. Nuala Allen. Tel/fax 045 404727. 40 ptchs. £3-£8. All year.
From Dun Laoghaire follow N4 & N7, then take N81. 15km S of Blessington turn L at Old Toll House pub. Site 2km.
On site/nearby: toilets, shwrs, laund fac, hook-ups, payphone, shop, pub, rstrnt.
189. Lakeside, Mountshannon, Co. Clare, Eire. Thomas Bottcher. Tel 061 927225; fax 061 927336. 40 ptchs. £6-8. May-Oct. 1st turning R past Mountshannon on the Portumna road, site signed.
On site/nearby: toilets, shwrs, laund fac, hook-ups, pay-phone.
190. Shannon Cottage, O'Briens Bridge, Co. Clare, Eire. Ann Hyland. Tel 061 377118; fax 061 377966. 21 ptchs. £7-£11. All year. Turn off N7 at Birdhill (R466) to O'Briens Bridge. Site 100m E of Bridge.
On site/nearby: toilets, ch shwr block, laund fac, hook-ups, pay-phone, campers' kitchen, pubs.
191. Lough Ree East, Ballykeeran, Athlone, Co. Westmeath, Eire. John Kelly. Tel 0902 78561/74414; fax 0902 74414. 40 ptchs. £2.50-£7. Apr-Sept. Take N55 off Athlone bypass, head N for 3km. Site behind stone clad house in Ballykeeran. On site/nearby: toilets, shwrs, laund fac, hook-ups, payphone, campers' kitchen, shop, pub.
192. Hodson Bay, Kiltoom, Athlone, Co. Roscommon, Eire. Bridge & Paddy Lenihan. 0902 92448. 35 ptchs. £6.50-£8. May-mid Sept. From Athlone go 3m on N61 twds Roscommon. Turn R at junction for Hodson Bay. 1m to site.
On site/nearby: toilets, shwrs, laund fac, hook-ups, payphone.
193. Hydeoute, Clonbur road, Cong, Co. Mayo, Eire. M. Waldron. 092 46086. 50 ptchs. £5-£7. Apr-Oct.
0.5m west of Cong on R345 (L101). On site/nearby: toilets, washing fac, payphone, shop, pub, rstrnt.
194. Renvyle Beach, Renvyle, Connemara, Co. Galway, Eire. Pauline & Michael Mortimer. 095 43632/43462.
36 ptchs. £4-£7. May-Sept. 12m N Eastr of Clifden on N59 (T71), turn west at Letterfrack via Tully Cross twds Renvyle. Site on R close to Connemara Nature Park. On site/nearby: toilets, shwrs, laund fac, hook-ups, payphone, shop, pub, rstrnt.
195. Tara, 4 Ballyquintin Road, Portaferry, Newtownards, Co. Down, N. Ireland, BT22 1RF. John Keating. 01247 728459. 60 ptchs. £2-£5. End Apr-Oct. From Portaferry take Cook Street, then Ballyfounder Road and along Ballyquintin Road to signed site entrance. On site/nearby: toilets, shwrs, hook-ups, pubs.
196. Round Lake, Murley Road, Fivemiletown, Dungannon, N. Ireland. Libby McLean, Dungannon District Council. Tel 01868 767259; fax 01868 767911. 12 ptchs. £5-£8. All year. From A4 Fivemiletown, follow signs. Collect keys from Valley Hotel, Main Street, Fivemiletown. On site/nearby: toilets, shwrs, payphone, shop, pub, rstrnt.
197. Atlantic 'n' Riverside, Easkey, Co. Sligo, Eire. Louis Smith. 096 49001. 50 ptchs. £4-£7, stay a week get 3 nights free. Apr-Sept. 26m west of Sligo off main Sligo/Ballina road, Site in centre of village; call at post office.
On site/nearby: toilets, shwrs, laund fac, hook-ups, payphone, campers' kitchen, pubs, shops, rstrnts.
198. Kinnego Marina, Oxford Island, Lurgan, Co. Armagh, N. Ireland. Paddy Prunty, Harbour Master. Tel 01762 327573; fax 01762 347438; mobile 0374 811248. 10 ptchs. £5-£6. Apr-Oct. Leave M1 at J10 for Kinnego Bay.
On site/nearby: toilets, shwrs, laund fac, payphone, pub, shop, rstrnt.
199. Gortin Glen, Glen Park Road, Lislap, Omagh, Co. Tyrone, N. Ireland. Omagh District Council. Tel/fax 016626 48108. 24 hard ptchs plus tent ptchs. £4-£7. All year. Off main B48 Omagh to Gortin Road, 7m from Omagh. Site signed. On site/nearby: toilets, shwrs, laundry room, hook-ups, barbeque, pubs, shops.
200. Springhill House, Moneymore, Co. Londonderry, N. Ireland, BT45 7NQ. National Trust, Patricia Law. 016487 48210. 20 hard ptchs plus lawn. £3. All year. On B18 to Coagh, between Magherafelt and Cookstown. House signed from Moneymore.On site/nearby: toilets, hand basins.
201. Dungloe, Carnmore road, Dungloe, Co. Donegal, Eire. Charles Greene. 075 21021. 25 ptchs. From £8. May-Sept. On N56 Dungloe to Glenties road, entering Dungloe look for Esso station, then signed to site.
On site/nearby: toilets, shwrs, laund fac, hook-ups, payphone, meals, shop, pub, rstrnt.

Real
Exploring **FUN ON THE WAY**

Ship's Log
Keep a log of your journey, with pictures and souvenirs. Make sure children know what kind of log you mean!

Nature Hunt
How many different types of leaf can you find? Shells? Birds? Or whatever.

Gardening Competition
Issue everyone with a paper plate. Prize goes to the best garden made on it from moss, stones, twigs, leaves, matchsticks, silver foil, (legally picked) flowers ..... or whatever.

Bookworm
Read the book you've always meant to read, or one you'd never dreamt you'd read. Write the one you've always meant to write. Read about the great explorers – Scott of the Antarctic will cheer you up on a chilly night in Chelmsford.

Hide and Seek
Another old favourite. Give kids whistles if they're going far.

REAL map-reading!
More to reading a map than knowing where to turn right and left. When the day's route's been planned, let everyone study the map for ten minutes, making notes if they wish. Ask them to describe what they expect to see along the way – undulating countryisde, or flat terrain? Woods or marshland? Landmarks, rivers, railway lines? Prize at the end of the journey for the best advance description.

Landmarks!
From your site, pick out five landmarks, major or minor.
Scramble their names into anagrams, and see who finds them first.

Official Artist
Learn to sketch and record your journey. Crayons and pastels are easier on the move than paints.

Crafty Kits
Neat little kits for all sorts of crafts are fun to try.

Can you name
twenty types of bird, nineteen capital cities
eighteen flowers, seventeen items of furniture
sixteen languages, fifteen rivers
fourteen types of cake, thirteen insects
twelve British cathedral cities, eleven meat dishes
ten cartoon characters, nine types of boat
eight folk songs, seven famous hymns
six butterflies, five Prime Ministers
four crime writers, three types of llama
two kings of Scotland, one type of poisonous mushroom
and can you devise a similar quiz?

Good old-fashioned I-Spy
Remember? "I spy, with my little eye, something beginning with H" – and the others have to guess what you've spied. Wonderful on camp sites.
If you've any neighbours, don't be rude about them (or if you do, do it quietly!).

Simple Entertainment
Radio, tapes (try talking books), board games, crosswords, word game books, quiz books.